# TALES FROM THE
# COUNTRY PUB

*Simple pub food from Devonshire shown on this postcard dating from 1910*

# TALES FROM THE
# COUNTRY PUB

## BRIAN P. MARTIN

DAVID & CHARLES

To my father, Albert,
one of the most caring and generous publicans ever

(Page 2) *The picturesque Boat Inn (see pages 57–62), situated at an ancient crossing place on the River Severn*

(Page 3) *A convivial early 1950s scene inside The Liverpool Arms, a small pub built into one of the twenty-eight towers of Conway's town walls*

(Page 7) *A refreshing pint for local workmen at East Anstey, Devon. The men, who were building Moortown Manor, are pictured outside the Froud Arms*

A DAVID & CHARLES BOOK

First published in the UK in 1998
Reprinted in 1999
Copyright © Brian P. Martin 1998

Brian P. Martin has asserted his right to be identified as author of this work in accordance with the Copyright, Designs and Patents Act, 1988.

A catalogue record for this book is available from the British Library.

ISBN 0 7153 0541 7

Printed in the UK by Butler & Tanner Limited
for David & Charles
Brunel House    Newton Abbot    Devon

# CONTENTS

# CONTENTS

# INTRODUCTION

Some of you who have already looked at the contents page of this book may be muttering, 'Where's my pub?' Given well over 80,000 establishments to choose from, this was always going to be a very personal selection, tempered by advice and suggestions from a very large number of pub owners and, more importantly, customers. Nor is this one of those numerous pub guides which dwell endlessly on the merits of real ale or old beams (important as they are); it is primarily a journey back in time through the wide-ranging experiences and anecdotes of the publicans themselves. But I have featured some pubs that are chiefly distinguished by their unique position or great history; and there is a selection of pubs from most regions.

In the end, I have not even included my own 'local', the sixteenth-century Dog & Pheasant at Brook. Much as I love the place as the hub of our small community – with its unpretentious mix of familiar faces, banter and gossip, quaint architecture and pleasant aspect opposite the village green – to have written about it could have invited 'big trouble' as I always tell the truth about people, friends or not!

Not surprisingly, given the passion for pubs throughout these islands, I have never received so many offers of help with book 'research', as innumerable chums drooled at the prospect of so many real ales. But, with the important exceptions of Yorkshire and Ireland, I alone have 'carried the liver'!

*The pub has long been the social centre of the village: this scene, in Torrington, Devon, shows a group of customers outside the Setting Sun. The brewer (with the barrel) was Jack Gilbert*

The importance of recording these tales cannot be overemphasised: we are losing so much so fast, as the kings of commerce have the audacity to tell *us* what *we* need. It's bad enough that so many colourful tenants have been replaced by dull, over-worked managers with insufficient incentive, but now, swamping us with 'themed' pubs adds insult to injury and brings the collapse of individualism ever closer. Furthermore, those great character landlords and landladies of yesteryear are dropping off their bar stools far quicker than they can ever be replaced. Sadly, the irreplaceable Mabel Mudge of Devon has already gone to parts no beer can reach, while one or two other publicans included here have clearly heard the bell for 'last orders'.

Much of the general history of licensed premises is included within the following chapters, while the rest has been done to death elsewhere and would take an encyclopaedia to repeat. Therefore you will not find detailed analysis of numbers here, but what you are given is a collection of tales from *real* individuals who have stood the test of time in a demanding role often not fully appreciated by casual observers. The beaming smile and cheery 'What's it to be then?' may be offered genuinely, but they frequently conceal so much anguish and hard work 'behind the scenes'.

My fascination with old pubs began in 1954, when I was just seven and my father took the tenancy of the Victorian-built Three Tuns, in Hampshire. As customary, he had to buy the fixtures and fittings as well as stock and he paid £7 a week rent to the old Brickwood's Brewery at Portsmouth, with a year's notice either side. Ours was but one of three old pubs almost within spitting distance along Elson's main road. Although we enjoyed the close company of the community, our village – like so many others – was already being swamped by the adjacent town, 'greater' Gosport. Nationwide, this was a time of rapidly increasing prosperity, when many years of virtual stagnation and the sorry aftermath of protracted war were being swept away by an ever more mobile population. Throughout the kingdom, thousands of pubs like ours responded to that unprecedented period of change, none more so than those in the country as the motor car brought them within reach of the masses.

We had the common set-up of the time, with two front doors – one into the typical public bar where 'working men' played darts and cards, the other into the 'lounge', where 'ladies' and 'professional men' paid a penny extra to enjoy a little more comfort and separation from the *hoi polloi* if they so wished. At the back of the lounge bar, and accessed via a side entrance into a corridor, was a simple hatched door – an evolution of the old 'bottle and jug', the 'takeaway' where old ladies would come for their sherry

*An early morning scene in Mitchells & Butlers' brewery yard in the days before the advent of the motor lorry*

and third-pints of gin, and where boys would return empty bottles for a few precious coppers, including screw-cap quart beers for a princely fourpence.

At the back we had the traditional 'family room', like a private parlour, with an antique table covered by a sumptuous gold cloth, a large dresser and a pair of antique vases on the mantelpiece. There grannies and children were 'parked' in enforced patience, with their egg flip or ginger beer, as well as the obligatory packet of Smith's crisps – the old ones with the salt separate in a twist of blue paper – while their providers played 'arrows' (darts) and downed pints of bitter or cheaper mild in the public bar. Everything was against a drab backdrop of brown and cream paint.

To the side of the pub we had extensive outbuildings, where certain long-standing customers were allowed to keep their Rileys and Austins and other old cars with running boards. They were never locked and I used to sit in them and admire their cracked red leather upholstery or walnut dash. Above me was a huge loft which, like the attic of the pub, was stuffed full of yesteryear's rejects, ranging from a very old claypigeon

*Stopping for refreshment at the Devonshire Arms: a loaded charabanc on a day out in the early years of this century*

*Busy scenes at a wine and spirit merchant's at the turn of the century*

spring trap once used by the customers to a framed Victorian photograph of the pub.

We did not have spittoons but our cleaner still threw down sawdust in order to take up the bar-floor slops more easily. Every morning faithful old Bill Jones knocked at the side door as reliably as the church clock, at 6am, but his pace was that of another century and his standards did not come up to those of my ex-Navy pater. Characteristically, my merciful father did not sack Bill but continued to give him his few shillings and went round after him without saying a word.

Similarly, the previous landlord was from another age. With nowhere else to go, dear old Bill Windibank stayed on to live with us – our accommodation above the pub being generous – and to help in the bar, eventually becoming a much-loved surrogate grandfather. He smoked untipped Senior Service, drank gin even as a nightcap and liked nothing more than 'a nice bit of fat bacon', yet he smiled on into his eighties. I'll never forget the time when he dropped a bottle of gin behind the bar, mopped it up with a used teacloth and was about to squeeze it back into a bottle when Father said, 'No!'

Regular bar food was virtually non-existent in those days, but if anybody wanted a plain Cheddar cheese sandwich in buttered white bread rather than one of the unwrapped Brazil's pork pies under a glass dome, then that was all right: Mother would oblige. And any man late for his dinner back home, because he stayed in the bar too long, could placate his wife with one of our boxes of Black Magic, Dairy Box or Weekend chocolates.

Every day, the man from Marsh's Bakery came round with a tray of 'surplus' bread and

cakes for our pigs, no doubt with spiritual encouragement from Father. Well, being a bit of a Bunter, I was always on hand to help the tray in – those delicious lardy cakes were never too stale for me!

As well as porkers, Father kept about 160 Rhode Island Reds and a dozen or so capons, which were always so much more delicious than any fowl you get now, whether boiled or roast. No wonder those birds went like hot cakes when Mother started offering quarters or halves in the bar. The eggs were popular, too.

Cleaning out the hen houses, weeding the large vegetable plot and sweeping up around the pub earned me £1 a week pocket money, a very generous sum in those days. Even so, I did help myself rather and over the years thought nothing of trying all the optics in the 'blacked-out' public bar while Father was occupied in the lounge, tending to the 'old school', who frequently knocked back Scotch into the small hours, sometimes running up sizeable 'tabs'.

Suddenly it was all change. To their mutual advantage, Father and the brewery agreed to 'modernise', putting in entirely new counters, mirrored shelving, furniture, furnishings and facilities, not to mention a record player! Everything was done to very high standards and, for the time, in the best possible taste. And everyone was delighted because in those days popular preoccupation with the antique and historic had yet to happen. But I did manage to scrabble around while the bar floorboards were being ripped up, to gather lots of old coins which had fallen down between the cracks over many decades.

The money came rolling in, of course, as more prosperous and upwardly mobile punters were persuaded to give us a try. Luckily old faithfuls such as Harry Ryves kept shuffling along to play Newmarket and dominoes in their usual corner. But all the old intrigue had gone for ever and the farthings I once spent on sweets were no longer available to bet on the cards.

By the early 1960s the business was booming, but by that time my parents had become rather jaded by the relentless pressure and Father's chest was persistently congested through inhaling so much smoke, so they took their wad into well-earned semi-retirement. But this story is not ours alone – it is one which has been reflected in countless other pubs throughout the land.

BRIAN P. MARTIN
*Brook, Surrey*

*The Bull's Head at Little Hallam, Ilkeston, sometime before 1903: note the licence for entertainment*

...that's worth a

# Worthington

# CALLING TIME ON THE CENTURIES
## The Oldest Pubs in the British Isles

Our native ale, made without hops, was brewed in villages and settlements as early as about 5,000 years ago, but it does not appear to have been sold from alehouses until the introduction of taverns by the Romans. When ale started to be brewed with hops (to improve flavour and keeping qualities), from the fourteenth century, it became known as beer and was sold in beerhouses. Over the ensuing centuries the terms alehouse and beerhouse became interchangeable.

None of Britain's earliest taverns and alehouses has survived, but there is some archaeological evidence, including drinking vessels found in London dating from about AD300. Being of pint and quart size, they suggest trade in ale or cider rather than wine. Most early alehouses were simply extensions to existing buildings, but some of the first inns were probably purpose built to provide accommodation as well as food and drink along established routes. As early journeys were often linked with pilgrimages, many early inns were built by the church.

*(above) The perils of cider drinking!*

By the end of the Anglo-Saxon period alehouses had already proliferated to such an extent that King Edgar, in about AD970, tried to limit the number in any one village, and also introduced graded measures. The pegs on the insides of wooden drinking vessels marked the limit for each drinker before he passed the vessel on to his companions and this gave rise to the expression 'to take someone down a peg or two'.

Eventually taverns, alehouses and inns became known collectively as public houses, or pubs, and a move to control them was made in 1495, when Henry VII gave local magistrates the power of closure. This was reinforced by an Act of 1552, which required alehouse keepers to obtain a special licence to operate. Further legislation and a shift in society's attitude steadily reduced the number of licensed premises. In 1577 there were 17,367 alehouses, 1,991 inns and 401 taverns in England and Wales, compared with some 78,000 pubs in the UK today. Allowing for the huge increase in population, the number of people per pub has soared from only 187 to about 1,029.

No one can say for sure which of our surviving buildings has been selling alcoholic drinks for the longest. Call them what you will – inns, alehouses, taverns or public houses – many have been rebuilt on the site of earlier hostelries and very few of those still standing have survived more or less intact. There can be little doubt that the old plaster, paint and panelling within innumerable antique establishments today conceal features of even greater antiquity. Many of these old buildings have been licensed premises for only part of their lives.

For the purpose of this book, there is the added problem of defining 'countryside'. Some of the oldest pubs now in towns were originally in open, undeveloped areas. Most of the earliest were built in towns, but many are in places which have since declined and now belie their former importance. Others were established along important routes, especially at key sites such as crossroads, embarkation points and river crossings.

The **Royalist Hotel**, at **Stow-on-the-Wold** in Gloucestershire, is so sure of its ancestry that it openly advertises as 'the oldest inn in England'. Behind the Jacobean façade of what is now a smart hotel in a chocolate-box tourist town stands the original mediaeval, oak-framed structure, which has been radiocarbon-dated back to AD947.

Built by a Cornish Saxon Duke named Aethelmar, the Royalist was a refuge along the Fosse Way and over the years it has seen many different uses. Once owned by the Knights of St John's Hospitallers, it was run as a hospice and poor house, subsequently an inn known as the Eagle and Child, as well as a porch house and holmlea, a court house, base for the Royalists during the English Civil War, and a post office. But for exactly how long it has sold drink we cannot be sure.

Many interesting discoveries have been made at the Royalist, including a pit for bear baiting beneath the coffee shop, a Royalist commander's letter, a tenth-century Saxon shoe and a tunnel that leads to the church in one direction and to Maugersbury Manor (nearly a mile away!) in the other. Still to be seen are the leper holes, the circular 'witches' marks' – to ward off evil spirits – on the huge stone fireplace in the dining room, and some of the exposed thousand-year-old timbers.

More cautious is the **Bingley Arms** at **Bardsey**, West Yorkshire, which only claims to be *one* of England's oldest inns, even though church records date it back to AD905

*Yet another pub with a claim to being 'the oldest inn in England': Ye Olde Trip to Jerusalem, Nottingham*

and the centre part of the existing building dates back to AD953. Furthermore, it is mentioned in the Domesday Book and alongside it was England's oldest known brewhouse, with records of brewers and innkeepers there from AD953. The first recorded keeper was Samson Ellis, whose family ran it right up to 1780, when Baron Bingley gave the pub its current name. Until then it had always been called the Priest's Inn, and the massive stone inglenook still contains a priest's hiding hole built after the dissolution of the monasteries in 1539, private mass being given for the gentry at that time.

Once connected with Kirkstall Abbey, the inn was used as a rest house for monks travelling to St Mary's of York. Later it was a stop for stagecoach passengers, adjoining buildings being used as stables. Also, from AD1000 it served as the local courthouse. Among interesting features still to be seen there are two expansion and contraction branches in the first-floor flues, which are perfectly preserved despite a reputed age of 700 years. The Dutch oven in the bar dates from 1738 (when the building was subject to major renovation and extension) and is one of few English examples in its original position.

The **Fighting Cocks** at **St Albans**, in Hertfordshire, is a later structure, dating from the eleventh century, but it is on a site traced back to AD795, though it may not have been used as an alehouse until considerably later. Some 400 years ago it was known as the Round House because of its unusual shape. In Stuart times the sunken area down from the bar, with its ring of comfortable seats, was a cockpit.

Another unashamed claimant to the title 'England's oldest inn' is the **Old Ferry Boat Inn**, at **Holywell**, in Cambridgeshire. Documents record that liquor was first retailed here as early as AD560, although experts estimate that the foundations are a century older. Part of the inn's granite floor contains a slab that is larger and protrudes further than those around it, marking the grave of a 17-year-old who was buried there in AD1050. Apparently she was a beautiful girl who committed suicide for the love of a local woodcutter, and she is said to haunt the inn to this day. To have the best chance of seeing Juliette you should go there on 17 March, the anniversary of her death.

This pub certainly had good reason to have been there for so long, as the operator of a ferry across the Great Ouse. Apparently one passenger who found time to pop in for a swift half was resistance leader Hereward the Wake, on his way to Cambridge during the Norman invasion of Britain. Although the arrival of modern roads made the ferry redundant, the pub still retains the ancient rights to take people across the river. But all this rich history nearly came to an abrupt end in March 1997, when the pub lost its entire thatch to a big fire.

Dating from 1590, the **Crook Inn** at **Tweedsmuir**, in the Borders, is said to be Scotland's oldest licensed inn, with a licence dating from 1604. Sitting by the old Edinburgh-to-Dumfries road, the inn was originally built to accommodate drovers. Once the kitchen, the bar has a huge central fireplace which you can walk all around. Robbie Burns knew the inn through his work as an exciseman and he wrote his poem 'Willie Wastle's Wife' while staying there.

Although an inn has stood on the site of Dublin's Brazen Head Inn since the twelfth century, the present building dates from 1668. Ireland's oldest surviving pub is **Grace Neill's Inn** built at the fishing port of **Donaghadee** in 1611, just three years after the establishment of the world's oldest whiskey distillery at Bushmills. With only twelve people in, the small original bar is packed, so a tourist extension was tacked on the back in 1993. However, the Russell family (who have owned the pub since 1973) have ensured that the place retains its great character. Most of the beams in the old bar are believed to be timbers from ships wrecked on County Down shores. The pub remains lively, too, with the locals often singing from the Irish folk song books or playing the tin whistles kept behind the bar. Originally called the King's Arms, the pub was renamed early this century after landlady Grace Neill, who died in 1916 at the age of ninety-eight. Some customers say that she haunts the place, being cross that her beloved inn has been altered.

Over the centuries, the pub has had quite a few famous customers, including the

*Grace Neill's, Donaghadee, the oldest bar in Ireland*

composer Franz Liszt, Thackeray, Dan O'Connell (the uncrowned King of Ireland), author Daniel Defoe (of *Robinson Crusoe* and *Moll Flanders* fame), English poet John Keats and Irish author and playwright Brendan Behan, who apparently spent more time in the pub than he did painting Donaghadee lighthouse, for which purpose he had been sent north. Tsar Peter the Great of Russia stayed there, too, when he took shelter from a storm on his way to Warren Point to study shipbuilding, and the upstairs 'Emperor's Room' still commemorates his visit.

One of the old customs at the King's Arms was for the landlady and her maids to kiss visitors on their arrival, which in the case of Peter the Great must have been both difficult and pleasurable as he was 6ft 7in tall and very handsome.

There have been less savoury associations, the County Down pub's pictures of guns reflecting long links with smuggling and horse thieving, in the days when Donaghadee was the main sea port to the Isle of Man and Galloway. Apparently a tunnel once led from the pub to the harbour, about 160 yards away, so that contraband could be moved without interception. However, the inn's main trade was with passengers embarking on the short sea passage to Portpatrick, often in escape from poverty and oppression.

# LIFE AT THE TOP ...

*In England's Highest Pub –The Tan Hill Inn of Yorkshire*

Not for nothing is the Tan Hill Inn's bar fire kept going twenty-four hours a day 365 days a year – 'except when a new grate is needed'. At a height of 1732ft (528m) above sea-level and on open, desolate moorland, it is England's highest and one of Britain's most remote and exposed pubs, and as such it is continually subjected to some of the most severe weather these islands have to offer. Magazine editor Robin Scott told me: 'When I was a local newspaper reporter there was always a race to be the first journalist to reach Tan Hill after heavy snow. Some twenty years ago I made it, but after I battled through I found the bar crammed with stinking sheep! When I asked the landlord about his most unlikely customers he said: "Well, they were out in the car park and I couldn't leave the poor things there, could I?" '

Life at Tan Hill has been so harsh – the frost sometimes even shattering spirit bottles – that most previous landlords (there have been many since World War II) have not stayed on for a second winter. One poor man there was cut off by snowdrifts for eleven weeks running and did not see a single soul to wish him happy new year until a shepherd passed by at the end of March! However, over the centuries there have been doughty exceptions, not least Fremmy Hutchinson, who liked the place enough to call his son Tan. But few have managed as well as the current owners, Margaret and Alec Baines, who have 'survived' there since 1985, even though it's taken them twelve years to get invited to a local party!

In her colourful and frank manner, licensee Margaret told me all about her bitter and wind-blown experiences as we sat in the bar one cool October evening, when there were only her family, their recumbent dog and three young walkers to share that cheery fire.

'So far, our worst weather here was in early 1985, only three months after we moved in, and we had to melt snow for drinking water. The ice was up to four inches thick on the windows, so no daylight could get through at all and to see anything we had to leave all the lights on even in the middle of the day.

'Financially it was a nightmare. The brewery lorries couldn't get up, but we weren't in any danger of running out of beer with only twelve customers in two weeks, and nothing would go off in that cold! The first people through were soldiers walking over from Hawes, and when they arrived all the beer lines running out from the garage were frozen: but believe you me, those twenty Army lads soon thawed 'em out.

'That same winter the lemonade froze out in store, shattering all the bottles, leaving solid blocks of drink and thousands of glass splinters. My husband said: "Can't we thaw 'em out, sieve liquid and re-bottle it?" So I said: "Don't even think about it, Alec."

'When we were completely cut off, two kind members of Kirkby Stephen Fell Rescue Team hiked for four and a half hours through the snow just to bring us papers and milk for

(above) *Snowbound! Arctic conditions at the Tan Hill Inn in 1934 and* (left) *the pub's position on 'open, desolate moorland…'*

daughter Kimberley's baby bottle. We were so surprised, and they only stayed for one quick drink as they had the same trek home to do.

'The snow often starts as early as September and can still be several feet deep on surrounding moors in late May. So it often takes people by surprise and I wouldn't like to count the number of motorists Alec's pulled out snow. Just on New Year's Day 1996 he helped over twenty! When Alec's been away tending to 'is sheep I've known it take 'im eight hours to get back just five miles. He won't give up and spends hours diggin' Land Rover out – 'e says it might get nicked, but who'd be out stealin' in that weather?

'That first year we were here, when the snow blower came through we thought we'd follow it down to get some fresh bacon and meat. But we stayed on a bit talking to someone and when we went to go back the blower had gone home and the road had already filled in again, to about 6ft deep at the sides. It took us four hours to do three miles with all the shovellin', and we had the three kids with us so it was really frightenin'.

'We had a bad time in 1990, too. Look at this extract in my diary for December 8:

"I came down to make the tea, opened the door to let the dog out and was met by a solid wall of snow. The whole pub at the front is an igloo. We can't open doors or windows – not that we're going anywhere or can see anything for the blizzard outside.

"Billy the barman came back from feeding the hens with a bucketful of frozen bodies which we thawed out in front of the fire, so now the bar's full of grateful birds. We haven't found the twenty ducks yet. So here we are with no electric, no water, no customers and no roof (under repair) but as much snow inside as outside. One thing Billy did say, he would let us have what water was left and he would tolerate drinking beer."

'For December 9 my diary continues:

"The kids have a great snowslide from the bedroom window onto what was the Land Rover and into a drift. They're cold but happy."

'Other times chickens get frozen to perch. One day Billy came in with one on his shoulder and we thought it were still alive. Our two budgies died of cold, too, or it could 'ave been smoke inhalation.

'The snow often blows in through cracks round doors and windows and we get big snowdrifts in the toilets. In 1990 snow came through the kitchen air vent, piled on the hood of the Calor gas stove, melted and put the burners out, so Alec blocked all entrances to the house with wads of hand-crushed snow. But even in those conditions six Pennine Way walkers came in, desperate for a beer. They stood in a row, holding the beer-line in their hands to thaw it out so they could have a pint!

'Thirty-foot-deep drifts are not uncommon up 'ere and we've had a few customers snowed in for up to five nights. Luckily they were drinkers. My worst nightmare is to be marooned here with a load of teetotal vegans with no money!

'But you know when it's really cold, as an interesting ceremony takes place in front of the bar fire, when farmers take it in turn to point their backsides at the heat, then move aside and pause before sitting down. Now that pause is very important because if the men sit down too quickly they burn their bums on their trousers.

'Unfortunately, some first-time visitors behave very irresponsibly in the snow. For example, this year a chap of about sixty-five came in when a real blizzard came on. He'd had a recent hip replacement and was soaking wet and cold, so we dried him out and offered him a bed. But he ignored our advice to stay and insisted on carrying on down to Frith Lodge, near Keld, where he'd booked in. "No, I'm a walker," he said, and off he went at about 6pm.

'Later on Frith Lodge phoned and said this chap hadn't turned up and they wondered if we'd seen him. So Alec said he'd go and look for 'im and went all the way to the lodge without any sign, so we notified police and fell rescue. Next thing there's about fifteen police cars outside, but the fell rescue vehicle found the man about eight miles down the road. He'd gone in the wrong direction, was knackered and had slight hypothermia. But he refused to go to hospital and still insisted on going to Frith!

'Then the local radio got onto the story, but this chap didn't have the decency to go on air to thank everyone who'd looked for 'im. He said 'e didn't ask anyone to come out, but if they 'adn't found 'im down there that night 'e'd 'ave been dead. And 'e didn't even make a donation to the rescue service or write to thank them!

'The wind is as bad as the snow, with slates flyin' off the roof all the time. One morning when Kimmy was eight and getting ready for school, she'd just been into the living room to get some things when we heard such a bang in there. When I went to investigate at first I couldn't open the door because of the strength of the wind. So I shoved as hard as I could and then saw that a slate had come down and shattered this 6ft plate-glass, double-glazed

*The interior of a typical old moorland pub towards the end of the nineteenth century: some remain relatively unchanged to this day*

window, and hundreds of splinters were embedded in the wall and the settee. If little Kimmy had still been in there she'd 'ave been dead!

'I gave up hangin' washing out ages ago. There's more of my knickers on Bowes Moor than anywhere else. Anyway, for 'alf year anythin' that stayed on line would be frozen in minutes. And if I tried puttin' out a sheet with even the smallest hole in, it would be shredded in no time.

'Our collection of hats in the office is marvellous. Most of 'em blow down onto a bit of fence at the bottom and their owners can't get down to 'em. Little ol' ladies with umbrellas – they're fantastic – they just get out their cars and fly! And there's no end to the number of car doors that's blown off up here.

'One day the wind was so wild it blew postman away – just picked all fifteen stone of 'im up and dropped 'im over there. Chickens get blown away as easily as feathers, and I think the council should put up a sign saying: "Beware of low-flying sheep!" '

With such exposure to the elements, it was not surprising that Everest double-glazing chose the Tan Hill for its television advertisement in the mid-1970s. In this, the popular broadcaster Ted Moult struggled across the adjoining moor to the pub, dropped a feather inside the newly installed windows, then paused while supping a pint to quip: 'This is the only draught you will find up here.'

The local council then said the old windows had been removed without planning

24

permission and demanded that the new ones be removed at once. Understandably, their decision was ridiculed in the national press, so the double-glazing remained in place. Subsequently, the Baineses had to do battle over other harsh planning restraints, such as in choice of building materials.

But snow, low temperatures and high winds are not the only weather hazards at Tan Hill. Sometimes the fog is so thick the Baineses cannot even see across the road. Also (surprisingly for England's highest pub) they have been flooded out.

'It was when Hurricane Charlie came through in the night, but I'm a heavy sleeper so I hadn't heard what was goin' on. In the morning I went down and when I opened the back door all this water came rushin' in. I tried to shut it out but the force of water stopped me, and there I was in me nightie with these campers lookin' on in amazement. Soon I was knee-deep in water with a river runnin' right through kitchen and bar. Fortunately it soon drained away.

'Later that day I was clearin' up in me wellies when this shooter came in. He was an oldish and respectable sort of feller and I said to 'im: "You 'aven't bin shootin' in this weather, 'ave you?" "No," he replied. Then I said: "So what do you do when it's cancelled? It must cost you a lot of money. I understand that they charge up to £3,000 a day to shoot on moor." So he said: "Excuse me, madam, but I don't pay to shoot – I own the moor! I'm the Duke of Norfolk. But while I'm here I'll have a ploughman's." So I slopped off through the water in me wellies to get him some bread and cheese, chucklin' away as I went.

'And while we're talkin' about shootin' I'll tell you somethin' – those grouse are such intelligent birds. They know that if they sit near the pub they're not goin' to get shot, so on a shoot mornin' we often have them perched on the porch roof, along the window sills and other places. They have their own language and sit there talkin' about all the stress they endure.'

But who on earth would want to live at Tan Hill, in what was described in William Camden's *Britannia* in 1586 as 'a solitary inn in the middle of a vast and mountainous tract'? Indeed, surveyors compiling the Domesday Book in 1085 stopped at Reeth, dismissing the area beyond, including Tan Hill, as 'wasteland'. And how did the Baineses end up there? Margaret explained:

'We're told there's been a buildin' on the site since the thirteenth century and it was registered as an inn in the sixteenth. It's been gutted by fire at least twice and we've made a lot of changes, includin' buildin' the seven-bedroom extension, but the 3ft-thick walls and stone-flagged floors are centuries old and the original bar and fireplace are much as they were when we came here and for years before that.

'The inn originally provided accommodation and refreshment for drovers and pedlars. But it's also in an area once important for lead-mining and coal-mining. The coal wasn't very good but was all that the poor Swaledale farmers could afford, and was important in fuelling the lead-smelting kilns of Arkengarthdale, especially when most of the area had been stripped of trees. So the inn was first called the King's Pit and the landlord also used to be the manager of a mine on Tan Hill.

'In the old days farmers would struggle up the dale to sell produce and then queue to fill their carts with coal for the return trip, often quenching their thirst in the pub while they

*Margaret Baines serves a thirsty young walker*

waited. Tan Hill's last mine didn't close till 1929, when improved and toll-free roads allowed better coal to reach the area at affordable prices.

'I was born at Keighley and lived with Alec in a nice little cottage at Gargrave, near Skipton. I was just a housewife working part-time as a barmaid at the Mason's Arms and Alec worked for the water board and farmed sheep at Malham. Then one night when I was makin' tea in the kitchen there was this programme on television about Tan Hill being for sale. So Alec said: "Let's go and look at it," as he was used to the rugged life out on the moor, but I said: "Don't be so stupid – you're teetotal and you've never pulled a pint in your life."

'In the end we went to the sale, where the auctioneer opened by saying: "I'm looking for eccentrics," and he got them! We'd decided to bid up to £82,000, but Alec's hand shot up for a further £500 – probably because I had my hand in his pocket – and we got it. At first we thought, oh God, what have we done? We had no spare money to speak of, just this lovely little cottage and only a month to pay the full sum. But within minutes of getting back home the telephone rang and we were offered first £5,000, and later £10,000 above our purchase price, so we started to think we were on a good thing. And luckily we sold our cottage quickly.'

When the Baineses moved in, people told them: 'You won't last two minutes.' The change certainly turned out to be 'quite a culture shock' for the family, especially for Margaret's three young daughters from her first marriage.

*Landlord Alec Baines and his dog beside the fire that never goes out*

'It was a round-trip of fifty miles just to visit the bank manager and eleven miles to the nearest groceries. The shop in Reeth used to deliver, but after that closed I had to take the pick-up to the cash-and-carry at Penrith – forty miles away. Fortunately all our food is delivered now, but we don't always keep a big stock of things. People say 'ow d'you get deliveries in winter, but I say if you don't 'ave customers you don't need owt.

'We're usually busy up to December and we have had over 200 people on New Year's Eve, many campin' on moor or sleepin' on the pub floor as well as in the proper beds. But so much depends on the weather. Last 31 December we had only seventeen, and twelve of those had been here since Christmas while the other five had walked up in snow.

'When we came, my girls were aged two, eight and fourteen and there was no special school transport. Kim went to primary at Langthwaite, nine miles away, and Kirsty twenty-two miles to Richmond, and just to get them on the right buses took me two hours and journeys totalling forty miles every day. Mind you, it didn't matter much in that first winter as they were snowed in at home for six weeks.

'For contact with the outside world we rely on a radio telephone with a 20ft mast. Our generator often fails, leaving us without electricity. When we moved in, our water was pumped over the ground from a nearby stream, so in summer it often dried up and in winter it froze. But after a while I got tired of carryin' buckets 'alf a mile into moor just to get water, so we called in a water diviner to find a new source and now our supply's pumped from a bore hole 168ft below ground. It cost £3,000 to install, but it was worth every penny.

'We also soon discovered that there's not much point in tryin' to organise sports and social activities such as darts matches and dominoes leagues in winter. There's not enough people close enough to rely on for a regular team of any sort, and even if you are brave enough to arrange something a blizzard's likely to blow up and prevent most people getting in or out.

'We play a sort of cricket in summer, but it's a bit rough is pitch! So most of our games are just silly ones played when there's a few in on a Saturday night, such as tryin' to climb all the way round inside of pub without puttin' your feet on the floor.'

Although the Baineses can go for weeks in winter without seeing a soul, in summer they are overrun by thousands. Many holidaymakers arrive by car or motorbike along the minor road from Reeth to Kirkby Stephen, but most are serious walkers, the pub conveniently being about halfway along both the 250-mile Pennine Way walk and the Coast-to-Coast walk from St Bees in Cumbria to Ravenscar on the Yorkshire coast, the latter route passing close by at Keld.

A record book shows that these visitors come from all over the world, most to 'get away from it all', to enjoy some of Britain's most spectacular scenery and, as one German wrote, to be 'near to God'. Many travellers have been known to break into a run when they top the nearby hill and see the inn below. They will find a welcome there at most times of day. Many years ago, when a Mr Pounder applied for a licence, Richmond magistrates said he could open whenever he liked as 'no one arriving there should be refused a drink'. This admirable concern for customers certainly continues, for on many occasions weather-beaten Alec has even dashed in from sheep-dipping – still in his wellies – and gone behind the bar to pull a pint of Theakston's excellent Old Peculier or Black Sheep for some desperately thirsty hiker.

With the nearest house some five miles away, only a handful of people are regarded by Margaret as true 'regulars', but there is one event that always draws many more folk from the dales – and beyond – to the pub. This is the annual Tan Hill Open Swaledale Sheep Show, which has been held in the last week of May since 1951. For this Alec erects special pens and Margaret puts on teas as well as a sit-down luncheon of hearty food such as pie and peas and, of course, Yorkshire puddings. And as far as many folk are concerned this is the 'Royal Show for sheep farmers'. The prize money may be only a few pounds, but to triumph here is very special, as shown when winner Tupp Hogg was auctioned at Hawes for £30,000.

The Baineses have never had to advertise for staff because so many visitors are besotted by the place and want to stay on to help. Some have remained for years; others have simply worked for their board over weekends. 'So many people wouldn't go home, I thought I might as well employ 'em as keep 'em for next to nothing.'

Some folk have been so happy at Tan Hill, returning year after year, that they have had their ashes scattered there. In 1997 alone there were four – and it has always been wives doing the scattering!

'There's definitely a ghost here, too. I've seen her. One winter lunchtime, when I was sittin' by the bar there with this local lad and it was snowin' and nobody else could get up 'ere, we saw this woman walk past. Then another time, when Alec and I 'ad settee in front

of bar fire as we knew nobody was comin' in, the best bitter pump suddenly went down all on its own – no word of a lie – and then went back up. I said: "Who did that?" Alec said: "I don't know – there's only thee and me here."

'We know who the ghost is – it's Susan Peacock, who was the landlady here from 1902 to 1937, when her husband Michael owned the pit. Her memorial is carved in stone at back of pub. She was a really tough character who hardly ever left the pub and always kept a loaded gun behind the bar and would shoot at people late at night if she didn't want 'em in. When she was about to give birth here and was asked which hospital she would go to, she is said to 'ave replied: "Nay – I was tupped here and I'll be lambed here, too."

'Susan's presence is never felt in the new end of the building, but sometimes she gets really upset if you make alterations to the old part, and then odd things happen like pictures crash down. One night there were about five of us sat round fire when this picture of local farmer Dick Metcalfe fell off wall for no reason at all. I said: "I bet somethin's 'appened to Dick" (who was eighty-four then), "otherwise why should his picture fall down?"

'Next day, when postman came up I said: " 'Ave you 'eard owt about Dick?" "Yes," he said, "he had a really bad accident yesterday – 'e came off a four-wheel bike and broke 'is shoulder." '

Today Tan Hill remains an important part of Yorkshire's rich heritage, but for a while it was claimed by Durham. 'For centuries it was in Yorkshire, but with the local government reorganisation in 1974 it was given to Durham. This was stupid because our road was cleared of snow by North Yorkshire, our dustbins were emptied by Richmond Council, my children went to school in Yorkshire and we have always sold Theakston's Yorkshire beer. The only direct link with Durham was that we were policed by them, and that needed a 40-mile round-trip from Barnard Castle. Fortunately, the accountants made 'em all see sense and pointed out that the roads to the pub were unreachable without passing through North Yorkshire, and it cost about £8,000 a year just to keep the access open. Also, it cost £7,600 a year to get our children to school! So we were delighted to be returned to Yorkshire in 1991.'

Since 1994 customers have been able to get married at the Tan Hill Inn, and by the end of 1997 the Richmond registrar had already conducted 27 weddings there. Such is the pub's appeal that couples come from all over Britain, and even from abroad. The first couple to wed there had actually met at Tan Hill, and another stopped off to get hitched while walking the Pennine Way, resuming their trek the morning after the ceremony.

At the time of my visit there was considerable excitement at Tan Hill as it was young Kirsty Baines's hen night and she was to be married there two days later. Sadly, she was due to move away and not one of the Baineses' six daughters had expressed any interest in taking on the rigours of Tan Hill, which was unfortunate as forty-five-year-old Margaret and fifty-eight-year-old Alec were understandably looking forward to putting their feet up a bit. But you couldn't criticise the girls for wanting an easier, more predictable life. Alec told me: 'The one big advantage in living at Tan Hill is lack of complaints from neighbours,' but Margaret had to concede: 'It's only a great place to live if you don't mind the constant smell of sodden Barbour jackets.'

# HALF-PINT
# AND HARD-PRESSED
### England's Smallest Pubs

One or two pubs claim to be England's smallest, but it depends on which way you look at it – or them! For example, it has been said that the bar space at the Nutshell, Bury St Edmunds, does not have enough room to swing a cat: its floor area measures only 15ft 10in by 7ft 6in. Yet large numbers of people have been squeezed in there on a number of occasions. In 1982, the sixty-man crew of the submarine HMS *Opossum* joined forces with locals to cram no fewer than ninety people into the Nutshell. They beat the twenty-three-year-old record of eighty-three set by two local rugby teams in 1959. But since then the number has swollen to an impressive 102 plus a dog!

The Nutshell also has a considerable number of artefacts. When it began life as a beerhouse, in 1873, the original landlord stuffed it full of antiquities. Many of those have long since disappeared but among those remaining at this Suffolk pub is a mummified cat

(above) *The Nutshell – said by some to be the smallest pub in England. Incredibly, 102 people
(and one dog!) have squeezed into the tiny bar – but not on this occasion!*

*(above) The lovely garden at the Smith's Arms and (left) The Nutshell at Bury St Edmunds*

swinging from the ceiling. It is reputed to have been walled up alive to ward off evil spirits, and it certainly seems to work as the only spirits now found at this Greene King pub are guaranteed to warm the cockles of your heart.

The bar floor area of the Nutshell is certainly smaller than that of another claimant, the Smith's Arms, in the Dorset village of Godmanstone. However, the Nutshell is a three-storey building, whereas the Smith's Arms is all on one level and its external measurements are only 39ft 6in long by 11ft 6in wide – including stone walls 2ft thick. So, in terms of volume rather than area, the Smith's Arms is certainly England's tiniest tot – in both town and country – and it is probably the smallest pub on the UK mainland, too, though in Ireland there are many minuscule bars which often double up as shops.

'Half-pint' it may be, but you always get full measures of honesty and entertainment at the Smith's Arms. Conveniently only 5ft 4in small, ex-jockey and landlord John Foster was always bound to fit in, but even this larger-than-life character has sometimes

*The tiny thatched Smith's Arms in 1904 and* (right) *the present landlord ex-jockey John Foster*

had to bend over backwards to accommodate everyone's peculiarities. Mind you, our host is not one to be trifled with.

Legend has it that the Smith's Arms was granted a licence by thirsty King Charles II, on the run. For centuries villagers have believed that when the king happened to stop at Godmanstone to get his horse shod at the smithy he asked for a drink, and when refused he granted the smith a licence on the spot. However, recent research has shown the story to be corrupt. The truth is that while the king and his associates were in flight in 1651 they were hidden by the blacksmith's son for twenty-four hours. After the restoration of the monarchy, in 1661 the grateful king not only raised the blacksmith – one Mr Farrier – to the rank of 'gentleman' but also granted him and his heirs a licence to sell wines, porters spirits and beers both in perpetuity and free of customs duty. Apparently this is the country's only pub to hold a licence by royal charter.

John and Linda Foster took on the Smith's Arms in 1981 and purchased the freehold from the Devenish Brewery in 1988. Previously, they had run the White Hart in Weymouth for nine years. They have been careful to ensure that the 1420 building has retained its great character, but certain improvements have been necessary. For example, some of the seating has been changed: a previous landlord, who had worked for a coach company to supplement his income, used old bus seats as part of the pub's furniture.

**Smith's Arms**

The Smith's Arms-The Smallest Public House in England, originally a blacksmith's shop; King Charles II stopped here to have his horse shod, he asked for a drink & the blacksmith replied 'I have no licence Sire', so there & then the King granted him one.

J. FOSTER

The place was certainly a great deal more rustic until recent times. A customer since the late 1930s, John Whittle, told me about the day when a farmer 'who was always half drunk' brought a cob into the tiny bar. 'He was hoping the horse would defecate. That was the sort of thing they thought a joke in those days. But it wouldn't have mattered too much if the horse had obliged as the stone floor wasn't carpeted then. I was only about fifteen at the time, and under-age, but neither the landlord nor the village police-man ever bothered me as long as I sat quiet. I also remember when the landlord locked the Yankee 1st Division out when beer was rationed during the war, to make sure there was enough for the locals.'

The Fosters now have relatively spacious accommodation as they live in the next-door cottage, which used to be the village shop. But up to the early twentieth century the landlord-cum-smith, plus whatever family he had, squashed into the tiny pub build-ing along with a walled-off section in which the horses were shod and another for the actual forge. The latter part is now the tiny pub kitchen, and as recently as when the Fosters arrived, food there was still being prepared on the back of an old door! Now hygiene is to the fore and Linda Foster is renowned for her wholesome, home-made, good-value dishes.

In the attractive bar, where I enjoyed a well-kept pint of excellent Ringwood bitter, John described some of the necessary changes to the building:

'We're very fond of this little pub and have given it a tremendous amount of love and care, whereas if you look at these old postcards you can see that most of the previous owners didn't give a damn.

'There is no roof space between the ceiling and the thatch – it's still just the old cow muck an' 'orse 'air under the paint. See here, where I tried to knock a nail in: bloody great lump fell out so I had to give that up. The building has a maximum height of 12ft but much of the ceiling is only about 6ft 2in high. Even so, we've had the tallest man in England – at 7ft 6½ in – in for a drink, and when no seats were available he was pre-pared to kneel to drink.

'Now when we came here that was an open log fire, and when the wind blew up this valley we tended to get smoked up. Yeh, there was often more smoke in 'ere than any-thin' else, and whoever came in sat right in front of it. An' what's the first thing people do when they sit in front of a log fire? They poke the bloody thing! So those people near it got warm but those who sat back 'ere nearly froze to death. Also, when they poked it all the sparks flew up the chimney and I thought we'd get the thatch alight. So that's why I 'ad that enclosed coal fire put in, an' it's been wonderful.

'Outside at the front those old forge bellows are replacements which I found. The original ones were so old they just fell apart when I tried to move 'em. And soon after we came 'ere I 'ad that wire netting put all round the bottom edge of the roof because visitors kept taking handfuls of thatch as souvenirs.

'Old Bob Warren, who used to make the cider up 'ere, told me it used to be flood-ed out in 'ere when the spring come up, an' sometimes that put the fire out, so they concreted underneath to stop all that. Course, the water table's very 'igh 'ere. And the whole village  is still on cesspits or soakaways.'

With only six tables, the bar cannot seat more than twenty-three people. However, there is an attractive garden setting, where people can sit at rustic furniture and feed the ducks on the River Cerne while admiring the hills behind. This can quadruple the number of customers, which is very important because the pub is an international tourist attraction, being mentioned in so many guides. However, not everybody is welcome, as John explained:

'What annoys me most of all is people takin' photographs and films without askin' permission. They come in 'ere with their bloody cameras snappin' away an' I say, "What d'you want to drink?" They then say they'll be back later, so I ask, "Why are you takin' the photo now, then?" The truth is they ain't got no intention of comin' back.

'Then there's those who park in our car park, set up their campin' stoves, 'ave a good fry up an' 'ave the cheek to borrow our salt and pepper but not buy our food! We 'ad one party 'ere who came in for 'alf a bitter and then set up this wonderful picnic in our

*Dorset pub clientele in 1934: 'the lads of Dorset', photographed in the Rose & Crown at Bradford Abbas. Their ages totalled 434 years*

garden, with boxes and boxes of sammies, wine and even champagne. Turned out it was this chap's fortieth birthday so they thought they'd use our tables by the river for their celebration. So Linda soon let 'em know that we needed those tables for people buyin' *our* food.

'Course, this whole area lives on tourism. We get coachloads come day after day all through the summer and they fill this place, so we don't 'ave 'em between twelve and two because of people 'avin' lunch. One chap came off the bus first an' 'e got to the bar, where I said: " 'Allo my mate – what d'you fancy?" An' 'e said, "I dunno – what shall I 'ave?" So I said, "What do you want?" Then again 'e says, "I dunno." So I says, "Well, please make up yer bloody mind – cos if you don't, all that other bus load's gonna kill you." But then 'e just turned round and shouted down to 'is wife: "What d'you want, love?" An' 'er exact answer was: "What they got?" So I said to 'im: "Look, you stand aside and while the others get served you can decide what you want." So that's what 'e did.

'With all the tables full and not much room down the middle, what we do here with a coachload is let them out behind the counter after they've been served. If they tried to get back out the front door there'd be chaos. Like this, with just me and Linda servin' we can do a coachload of forty or more in about twenty minutes, an' that's sellin' post-cards an everythin', too.

'Once we 'ad a ladies' coach come, and they was a bit elderly so to make it easy for 'em I said to the first one: "Now look, darlin', when you've been served come out through the back 'ere and go down the side." But with that she called out to the others: "We've got to go out the back and down the side." An' before I could stop 'em they all trooped past without getting their drinks, because they thought they 'ad to be served elsewhere! Next minute they were all comin' in the front again. I 'ad a good laugh over that.

'Sometimes lorries can be trouble, when they rocket through the village and clobber the edge of our house, takin' the gutters off. Cars used to be a problem, too. When they came from the north they couldn't see the pub, with the house in the way, and when they suddenly spotted it they'd screech to a halt, sometimes rammin' into each other. That's why I had the pub sign put on the end of the house.'

On top of all these problems John has had to cope with increasing pain from a neck injury which required metal plates and forced him to give up the turf. So it was not surprising that in his sixtieth year he was thinking about retiring and put the pub on the market. But there is no doubt that for most of the time he has been more than happy at the beer-drinkers' Lilliput. As he told me: 'If you've got lovely people in, the pain doesn't hurt.'

# THE MOST UNSPOILT PUB

## *The Harrow at Steep, in Hampshire*

The fact that the Harrow, in the straggling village of Steep, was named by the *Good Pub Guide* as the 'most unspoilt pub of the year' in 1996 was particularly remarkable because a major road roars past almost on its doorstep. Fortunately, thanks to an embankment, the new Petersfield bypass cannot be seen from the pub and the Harrow enjoys almost as tranquil a setting as it did hundreds of years ago. Indeed, the pub has been partly saved because the new A3(M) cut off some of its feeder roads, making it even more difficult to find. But it is largely the long-term care of the current licensee's family that has preserved the timeless atmosphere of this very relaxing place.

Although Ellen McCutcheon was born at the pub, on 21 October 1929, it was well into 1997 before her name appeared over the door as licensee, following the death of her husband Eddie. Yet no one has done more – or should I say *less*? – than she has to retain the pub's character. One afternoon Ellen and I sat in the tiny public bar to discuss the past, in surroundings which looked virtually unchanged since the nineteenth century, if not earlier.

Although the McCutcheons have found many clues, such as the wattle and daub exposed while decorating, no one knows exactly how old the pub is, but there has been

*(above) A family concern. Pictured outside the Harrow are (left to right) (back): landlord A. M. Dodd, Mick Triggs (customer), Haden Dodd, Eddie McCutcheon, Bill Triggs (customer), Dick Guard (customer); (front) Elsie Everett, John Dodd, Annie Dodd, Ellen McCutcheon*

a building (intermittently used as an inn) on the site since at least 1608, when vestry meetings were held there. Its very secluded position now seems rather odd, especially as there were few locals to serve over the centuries before motor cars vastly increased the catchment area. No doubt the pub was strategically placed on the old drovers' routes, and it is said that land behind the inn once served as a pound where cattle could be left safely while their minders slaked their thirst. Certainly, a number of roads and old lanes still meet here and may once have been part of the route between Petersfield and Alton, as well as to other important centres such as Farnham's corn market.

Early travellers would have taken refreshment in the heavily beamed public bar, in the oldest part of the building, with its tree-stump stools burnished by innumerable bums around a huge inglenook fireplace, floor tiles laid straight onto earth, built-in wall benches, just two scrubbed tables, pine wallboards and smoke-veneered walls. This is where tobacco chewers would have used the green pottery spittoons which Ellen found in the shed, whereas those who could afford to puff on pipes and cigars would relax in the other bar, long known as the smoking room. This slightly larger bar may be mainly Victorian but is equally inviting, with a hotch-potch of old furniture and wall-mounted cases of birds (including a corncrake) collected by Ellen's grandfather. Wisely watching over all is 'Marge the owl, which was Grandad's pet, but she kept flying away so he had her shot and stuffed'. In both bars the walls are adorned with old photos and paintings of the pub and its customers; beams are festooned with hop bines from nearby Selborne and the tables are beautifully decorated with garden and wild flowers.

There is no noisy jukebox, gaming machine or piped music to spoil the simple art of conversation or concentration on dominoes or cribbage. There used to be a piano in the smoking room but, as Ellen told me: 'The pub cricket club took it up to the barn for a concert and it was left there. But it doesn't matter because nobody can play it any more and they don't have the sing-songs like they used to. Anyway, we needed the extra space for seating. There is an 1880 polyphon in there, but people used to pinch the perforated metal discs so now that's not played either. It was a wedding present to Mother from the founding headmaster of Bedales School, where my parents worked when they came to the area.'

*'Rogues gallery': customers outside the Harrow with landlord Eddie McCutcheon (back, second from right)*

The informal pub garden is delightful, too, and some of it is left to nature, with self-setting wild plants such as teasels to attract wild birds such as goldfinches. Other wild plants, including campions and

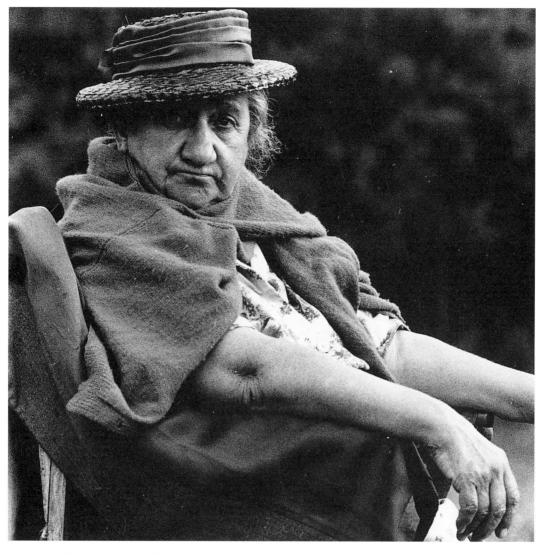

*Ex-landlady and suffragette Annie Dodd (formerly Annie Oakley) relaxing in the pub garden*

orchids, were rescued by the McCutcheons from the path of bulldozers building the bypass.

When Ellen was born, her parents rented only part of the pub as living accommodation. Her father, Arthur Dodd, took the licence in 1930, under the Luker Brewery of Petersfield. When Luker's College Street premises burnt down, in late 1933, Strong & Co of Romsey became the new owners and drinks suppliers to the Harrow. Annie Dodd became licensee in 1958, on the death of her husband, and Eddie McCutcheon took over some twenty years ago. He and Ellen bought the freehold from Whitbreads in 1990 and now Ellen runs the pub with the devoted help of her two unmarried daughters, Claire and Nisa.

I asked Ellen if her family had deliberately set out to remain in a time-warp. 'Oh no,' she said in her unassuming way. 'When you are young, things just happen and you don't think about them. Then, as time goes on, people point out that you have more and more of a treasure, so you are increasingly inclined to leave it as it is while most other places just follow the trends. Sometimes we get people who have not been back here since the war, and they are amazed to find it just the same.

'In fact there have been a few changes this century. In this public bar the lower wall-boards were almost black before they were stripped and Uncle Jack said that the little counter and serving hatch may have been put there in about 1910. Also in here, we used to have a much smaller Victorian fireplace. When we went to sweep the chimney the rods went up and up and never came out the top. So my thirteen-year-old brother, Haden, just about managed to climb up through the narrow flue to investigate. He was gone ages and one of our regulars was terribly worried. But eventually Haden returned safely and told us that the rods had just gone round and round in the great big space behind. So we took the Victorian fireplace away and exposed the large inglenook which you see now.

'Some seventeen years ago the authorities wanted us to have indoor loos, saying that the outside ones, across the lane, were unhygienic, but they didn't realise that people *liked* it that way. Also, this would have involved knocking the two bars into one and doing away with the barrels behind the bar. Instead of the beer being served straight from the wood, it would have been pumped from a new store outside. And once you start to change things you go on bringing in one new thing after another till you're just like everybody else. Anyway, our customers banded together and got the council to back down.

*The Harrow in the early 1950s*

'Mind you, we're on mains water now and it's lovely to have flush loos. My poor father had to empty the earth closets here, dig a hole, bury the contents and start all over again – day after day. But the piped drinking water we get now tastes awful and spoils your cup of tea.

'We thought the motorway would ruin us and fought to have it the other side of Petersfield, but us locals lost that one. Anyway, we decided it wasn't going to change anything and we did get compensation from the Ministry of Transport. Over the years the trade built up nicely, and Sunday lunchtime was always heaving, but this year (1997) things haven't been so good, and we think it's the introduction of Sunday shopping that's hit the country pubs.

'Of course, we've had to do more food, as people expect that now when they go out for a run: it's the motor car that's made the country pub. When most of the customers were local farm workers who either walked or cycled over and only wanted a drink, all we did was the odd cheese roll. Now we offer simple but good old-fashioned food such as ploughman's lunches and sandwiches, with salads and the occasional quiche, and something hot in the evening. And I've been cooking the same soup and boiling our own smoked hams for about forty years, ever since Mother showed me. It's the ham juices which make such good stock. We still cook on the old Rayburn and don't have gas or a microwave, but Nisa does much of the food now. She also makes our own sweets, such as treacle tart. And we often use our own eggs and whatever vegetables we happen to have in our kitchen garden. There's plenty of room out here as we've bought a couple of fields, which probably used to belong to the pub anyway, as the old wills suggest that the former owners had quite a big acreage.

'Our lighting used to be by paraffin lamps, which were very bright and warm and a bit dangerous: if you slammed the bar door – whooosh! – they'd flare up and burn a black hole in the ceiling. We always kept a big barrel of paraffin in the stable and people from roundabout would come down to buy it.'

In keeping with the pub's timeless feel, the McCutcheons have 'never thrown anything away'. Among the most intriguing records is a big, old account book showing how much money customers owed to Ellen's father. Of course, it would be imprudent to give examples here as some debtors or their relatives may still be alive. But Ellen did stress that her family frequently lost out. 'If someone owed for a pint costing 1s 9d, they'd often give you something like two marrows worth only sixpence, or a bunch of flowers when you already had a garden full!'

Equally fascinating are the old accounts with the brewery, which show not only much lower prices but also how slow some were to change. For example, from 1910 to 1917 the rent for the pub remained at just £2 10s quarterly, paid on the traditional quarter-days of 25 March, 24 June, 29 September and 25 December. This may be compared with an annual rent of £3 7s 6d plus 10s land tax, which remained unchanged from 1800 to 1832, which was surprising stability when the country remained deep in debt through the Napoleonic wars.

In 1910 the drinks prices paid by landlord C. Coffin to the Luker brewery included 1s a gallon for XX beer, 2s 6d a dozen for half-pint bottles of 'ale', 1s 2d a crate for stout,

(above) *The Harrow's spirit and ale account for December 1933 and January 1934, when the Strong brewery took over from Luker and (right) Uncle Jack Oakley who always sat in the porch, and was bought many drinks*

1s a gallon for cider, 15s a gallon for gin, 18s 2d a gallon for rum, 21s 2d a gallon for Scotch or Irish whisk(e)y and 27s 2d a gallon for brandy. In 1917 XX ale was up to 1s 6d a gallon, supplied in 36-gallon barrels, and XXX was 2s a gallon. By 1934 XX ale was up to 2s a gallon, while XXX cost 3s 1d a gallon and XXXX 4s 2d a gallon. The price of stout was well up, to 6d a half-pint bottle, while whisky and rum were now running equal, at 11s a bottle.

Daily takings in the 1920s averaged only £1 10s to £4, but often exceeded £5 on Sunday. There was little improvement in income during the 1930s, forties and fifties, so Arthur Dodd could never afford a car and often had to do other work to support the family, as did Ellen and her husband during their younger days.

'We used to have some really poor customers, some of the worst off coming from Village Street, in nearby Sheet. When I was a paper girl the houses there still had dirt floors and were packed with large families. It was a really rough place, but now it's all tarted up and elegant, and they call it a mews. How the farm workers who used to live there always seemed to find money for beer I do not know, but a lot of them did get free potatoes, milk and wood from their employers.'

The Harrow has had a wide variety of customers, including the actor Alec Guinness, who lives nearby. A lot of people have written comments, sometimes about each other, in the pub's 'Book of Quotations'. One, dated 26 March 1990, reads: 'In December Malcolm

[Clements] befriended a young actor visiting the pub and advised him to "try and get a proper job and a haircut". Four months later Daniel Day-Lewis received an Oscar.'

With such a varied clientele, I wondered if Ellen had encountered much snobbery. She told me: 'Not in my time. Of course, you get the odd trouble-makers or know-it-alls, but they don't get anywhere because everyone's treated the same here. I won't stand any nonsense from anyone.

'That reminds me – some people used to stick a poker in their beer to warm it up, making it all froth up and go lovely. Nobody could ever say it was unhealthy because the poker was red hot and killed off any bugs. But one or two who's tried it in recent times didn't know you shouldn't touch the bottom of the glass, and of course they cracked it.

'We've had lots of real characters among our regular customers, including my uncle, Jack Oakley. He was really old-fashioned with those long side whiskers and always sat out in the porch reading the paper, so when people came in they'd say: "What a marvellous old boy out there – give him a drink on me." But when they heard the cost they weren't so pleased, because Jack always drank a double shot of whisky and a Final Selection [strong beer] on top!

'If Uncle Jack was on his own in the bar he'd be quite happy to serve someone for us, as long as it was simple. But when this new lager was introduced he met his match. This man came in and asked for a Tuborg on ice, but poor old Jack couldn't understand what he wanted, so he came rushing out to me in the kitchen, saying: "You'd better come – there's a chap out 'ere wants two buggers on ice"!

'My father was a great character, too, and certainly liked a bit of fun. Every year he dressed a guy and put it out the front for 5 November. But one night he changed places with the guy and called out "Boo!" just as one of our regulars was walking past. The poor man was frightened to death.

'Another time Father caught this rat in a wire cage and Grinner (Bill) Greenaway, a keen dog man and puppy walker for the Cowdray Hunt, was in the bar all evening boasting that his dog could kill it. He was always saying that Flossie the spaniel was a real trick dog and he'd sit her in the corner of the bar with glasses on and a pipe in her mouth. So Father took the cage outside and everyone formed a circle to watch. But when the trap door was opened, out fell a lump of bread and Flossie jumped on that while the rat ran through Joyce Blake's legs and escaped. I don't think Grinner ever lived that down.'

Had those old characters been around today, they would be delighted at the way in which their old drinking place has been preserved. And if they scoffed at some of the few changes which have been forced upon the Harrow, then that would be understandable. In particular, Ellen told me:

'We used to write our drinks order on Sunday, catch the four o'clock post on the corner, and without fail the beer and so forth was delivered from Strong & Co of Romsey on Tuesday morning. Now the brewery telephone us on Thursday and enter our order into their computer, but the drink is still delivered on a Tuesday! Nothing much has changed for the better, has it?'

# BRITAIN'S MOST REMOTE PUB

*The Old Forge, Inverie, Western Highlands*

Geographically, the Old Forge at Inverie, on Scotland's west coast, is still regarded as Britain's most remote pub. Nestling at the foot of the mountains, on the coast of Knoydart's peninsular wilderness, it is 107 miles from the nearest city – Inverness – and has no access by car, the closest inland road being twelve miles away as the crow flies. Any local wanting to try another hostelry would either have to take the 45-minute ferry crossing to Mallaig or brave the daunting walk to Glenfinnan – seventeen miles away in an impossible straight line! However, if you take communications in their widest sense, then this pub is no more cut off than the rest of us because it now enjoys all the facilities of the electronics era, not least through access to the next-door estate office's fax machine and the Internet.

Such facilities have certainly proved their worth to Aberdeenshire-born ex-soldier Ian Robertson, both in owning the pub for the last four years and in his continuing job as manager of the Knoydart Peninsula Company's 17,500 acres. Knoydart is international-ly renowned for its deerstalking (with red deer up to 21 stone), and rich, busy clients require instant communications when booking for sport and accommodation.

Fortunately, the Western Isles enjoy a fairly mild climate, and during his first five years at Inverie Ian experienced lying snow at sea level just once. During the same period he was only 'marooned' on one day, when a persistently strong westerly prevented him from getting out to the estate's own boat.

The main weather threat is to Inverie's electricity supply, which was installed with the hydro in 1974. Lightning brings the power cables down fairly frequently, and then Ian has to rely on the pub's own generator. Also, they have sometimes run out of water as the area has been remarkably dry in recent years, but then who cares with plenty of beer on tap!

When I visited I took Bruce Watt's thrice-weekly ferry from Mallaig, in the company of a sheepfarmer, three hikers and local minister Ben Johnstone, making his fortnightly visit. Also on board were the village's post and newspapers plus a whole assortment of supplies ranging from a box of cauliflowers to lengths of timber, bags of sand and even a new saw.

*Landlord Ian Robertson and neighbours unloading supplies from the ferry at Inverie*

As I admired the local seals, Ben Johnstone explained that for a long time the Knoydart area remained a huge preserve of Catholicism, as its remoteness had protected it from the Reformation. The existing church building at Inverie was Church of Scotland but is now a private house, so Ben has to do his ministering in the little library just along from the pub, post office and shop. 'However, a good focal point is still provided by the school, even though it has only five children, and not so long ago the full-time teacher had only two pupils!'

The pub, too, is now an important focal point, but up to the last war this Victorian building was a forge, as a considerable number of ponies were once used on the land, as well as for sport and transport. With a current population of only about fifty, it is hard to believe that the wild Knoydart peninsula supported some 2,000 workers before they were shipped off to Nova Scotia during the highland clearances of the 1850s. Now the population of Inverie village itself is only about twenty.

When the forge closed, the building became the local working men's club. Ex-manager Dave Smith, who came to Knoydart from the Home Counties and still has a remote croft there, told me that the club used to open from six to ten Monday to Saturday evenings but only on one lunchtime – Saturday, when they did pie and beans. Some locals still refer to the Old Forge as 'The Club'.

By 1981 the population had become too small to sustain the club. Also, in those days there were very few visitors, with access remaining difficult for walkers. As a result, the old forge became a pub, and since Ian Robertson took over it has gone from strength to strength. With so many fishermen and other folk now prepared to come by boat, on 'theme nights' there can be over 150 customers – treble the entire peninsula population!

Nowadays the Old Forge's clientele is truly cosmopolitan and classless, ranging from three resident Knoydart millionaires and celebrities such as Tom Maclean and impresario Cameron Mackintosh, who have come to find peace, to 'old money' titled folk; from New World travellers tracing their roots, hikers, stalkers, anglers, and holidaymakers staying in the hostel or part-restored 'big house', to farmers, ghillies, professional fishermen, fish farmers, foresters, Knoydart estate workers and the lifeboat crew, which includes the minister. Also, in recent years there have been many more yachtsmen as Ian has put down an initial seven moorings. There was even a stag party from London. When they arrived the 'stag' was not stalked, but he was shackled to a ball and chain and the key posted to his girlfriend: yet the lad showed great spirit and still managed to climb one of the Munros, to 3,000ft!

Police visits are rare, there being no local bobby. Crime has been non-existent so officers generally only come on routine firearms licence checks. As a result, the locals may be rather relaxed when it comes to MOTs, but then there are only seven miles of single-track hard road on the entire peninsula, and they don't really go anywhere, merely to a few scattered houses around the coast. Most customers walk over or come by boat, though there have been rumours about ships being rammed on the return run!

As the pub is so important as a social centre, Ian exercises a degree of discretion when it comes to the law.

'We've often had whole families in for a cup of tea while waiting for the mail boat, for example, and it would be cruel not to allow the children in the bar on a cold day. Also, some community events inevitably attract a lot of youngsters who need diversion from what can be a very quiet life.

'The most popular of all local events is our annual Highland games, held on the beach near the pub in August and known locally as the "alternative games". Most modern so-called Highland games are geared to tourism and a bit plastic, so we like to inject a bit of old-fashioned fun. As well as more traditional events such as tossing the caber, a hill race, tug o' war and a pipe band, we have a raft race, tossing the boat and a bungee run. In the latter, a competitor is tied to a stake on the beach and lunges forward as far as he can, trying to reach first a can of beer and then, if he's really strong, a bottle of Scotch.

'For the games I put a beer tent on the beach, and as the event attracts so many young-sters I did consider literally limiting the tent to beer. But then the people told me that if I didn't supply whisky for the Mallaig fishermen they'd bring their own and things would be more likely to get out of hand. As it is, if you don't get up to the pub before the games finish you won't get in the door as half of Mallaig comes over.'

Being a free house, the pub has had a succession of guest ales. I tried the excellent Red Cuillin and Black Cuillin from the Isle of Skye Brewery, established by two teachers in 1995. The brewery was also about to produce a special beer for the Old Forge, to be called 'Knoydart Appeal' and geared to the November 1997 launch of the Knoydart Foundation. Following examples such as the island of Eigg, and set up by concerned

*Despite its remote situation the Old Forge attracts many musicians and customers*

organisations and individuals, the appeal aimed to raise £1.5 million to 'shake off the dead hand of absentee landlords' through buying and 'saving' the Knoydart peninsula, often described as Britain's last wilderness. Another of the Skye brewery's specials was called 'Extortion Ale', produced in 1996 to highlight the campaign against the new Skye Bridge tolls.

Although none of the small number of locals has expressed interest in working in the Old Forge, Ian has never had any trouble in getting staff. At the time of my visit the place was manned by a charming New Zealand girl, a Canadian and a Glaswegian, just the latest in a string of youngsters with a taste for adventure.

Nor is it difficult getting entertainers. Ian simply places an advert in the *Oban Times*, offering musicians free food and accommodation if they will come over to play. The response has been terrific, with as many as seven different fiddlers on one night, including celebrities such as Duggie Maclean.

The pub's visitors have also included a large party trying to protect the son of a celebrity from a fanatical religious sect. They certainly found somewhere out of the way, where for several months they could rehabilitate the young man without much risk of interference. They were able to spend much of their time in the pub while their charge wandered around at will: no way was he going anywhere!

51

# STARRING ROLE

*Britain's Most Filmed Pub – the Red Lion, Langthwaite*

Although it bears the commonest pub name in Britain, being one of about 630 so called, Langthwaite's Red Lion is a real star. With its simple old-world charm and attractive surroundings in a largely unspoilt North Yorkshire village, it has been filmed probably more than any other pub in the country. The full-length films and television programmes in which it has featured include Walt Disney's *Escape from the Dark*, BBC 2's *A Woman of Substance* and *Hold the Dream*, Tyne Tees Television's *Andy Robson* and *Dales Diary*, the BBC 1 children's serial *Century Falls* and (from 1977 to 1990) the highly successful BBC 1 series *All Creatures Great And Small*, based on the life of Yorkshire vet James Herriot (created by writer J. A. Wight).

The publican, too, has sometimes played a part in these films, along with other villagers. Landlady Margaret Winkfield, who passed the licence to her daughter Rowena in 1979, had a small part in *All Creatures Great and Small*, as did her late husband, playing dominoes in the bar. But Margaret was no stranger to theatrical life. Born in 1914 in Preston, Lancashire, and educated in London, she joined a ballet company in 1926 and later studied at the Slade. She described some of the scenes now immortalised in framed photographs hung on the bar walls at the Red Lion:

'With *All Creatures Great and Small* I soon got to know the BBC's filming routine so well they didn't bother with getting in extras from outside, but simply rang me at the pub to say how many men, women and children they wanted for the next programme. I also had to measure the inside leg of every man and boy before they brought the costumes up! And I provided a room at the back where they could carry out their routines, such as doing their hair and make-up.

'All the actors used to drink here, including Robert Hardy, Christopher Timothy and Peter Davidson. Robert often used to sit in this corner and go to sleep because he was so tired, but he was quite happy. Chris always sat there with a bag of toffees which he'd offer round, and often leave the remainder behind; but he always had a new bag when he came in again.

'Gradually we got to know each other very well and had a lot of fun. In one episode I was surprised to hear it said that the landlady of the Red Lion – then Rowena – was having an affair with a pig farmer! Then I discovered that Robert Hardy had altered the script as a joke.

'The pub was never changed much for the filming and we nearly always kept our real name, but sometimes they made the building look older outside. For *Escape from the Dark*, which was about a mining disaster and the last film that Alastair Sim made, the Disney team painted all over the white windows with a grimy colour, and they said

*Filming for Disney's* Escape from the Dark *at the Red Lion, Langthwaite*

*Margaret with her daughter Rowena, selling everything from batteries to books – as well as beer!*

they'd put it right afterwards, but it took quite a performance to make them act. To compensate for the nuisance they promised us a television aerial to improve our reception. However, this hadn't arrived by the first day of filming, so my husband told them that until the aerial was installed he was going to make their filming look silly by leaving his modern car in full view on the forecourt, which he did. As a result we had that aerial within a day.'

Not surprisingly, all this publicity plus a steady increase in tourism brought many more people to the pub. Not all were welcome.

'We bought the pub when my husband retired as a headmaster in 1964, and as we were able to pay for it outright we were never really interested in turning it into a great money-maker. We simply wanted to inject our own personality and create a warm atmosphere where we could sit and relax with the locals.

'The place was very run down when we arrived, as the previous owners seemed to go by the principle that the locals liked it rough. This was just at the time when pubs generally were starting to change quite a bit, customers were expecting more comfort and to be able to get bar meals. So, gradually and as diplomatically as we could, we tidied the place up. This didn't go down too well with some of the locals and we certainly went through a quieter time, but gradually the customers drifted back as they realised that this was the way things were going. But we never really modernised the place and it's still much as it was when we arrived.

'Soon after we moved in the local policeman came up to introduce himself and said:

"I hear you have three daughters." "Oh yes?" I replied. So he said: "Well, I suggest you tie them to the table legs because there are very few women in the dales." And he was right! So we had the situation where, say, an 18-year-old lad would come in for only half a pint to get the door open, and then quite a few more young men would slip in just to have a look at the daughters.

'The stock had been run down, too, with just the basic spirits, such as whisky at 2s 6d a shot, along with draught Newcastle Exhibition beer at 1s 10d a pint, Newcastle Starbright at 1s 8d and Younger's Tartan at 1s 6d, plus Newcastle Amber in bottles. Gradually we increased the range of drinks and made sure they were always in fine condition.

'At first there was virtually no demand for food, and I'll never forget the first time we made a sandwich. Instead of asking for something simple like cheese, this man wanted bacon, so it took three of us to prepare it – one to go out and buy the rashers, one to fry them and one to serve. But we had a good laugh about it afterwards.'

Margaret soon increased the range of food available, often using her own fresh eggs and vegetables, and she gathered wild strawberries to garnish tarts for afternoon teas. With skilled preparation of mostly traditional dishes, Margaret soon had a reputation as an excellent cook and in 1970 – only a few years after that first simple sandwich had been served – the Red Lion was included in the prestigious *Good Food Guide*. Further entries were to follow, but all was not well.

'After a while we declined inclusion in the guide. We were constantly booked up for meals six weeks ahead and it was obvious that we wouldn't be a quiet country inn for much longer. The catering was starting to overwhelm us, which was silly as we weren't in it for the money and we were being denied the peace we wanted.

'I did have certain rules, such as asking all men to take their hats off if they didn't do it straightaway. This started when people came in here wearing those with rude slogans, like you get on a day trip to Blackpool. Everybody has their own taste, and if someone doesn't like what we do then they're free to go elsewhere.

'Some people can be very pretentious and we encountered a lot of snobbery when we were in the *Good Food Guide*. That's partly why we got out of it. I didn't want people coming in and saying things like "Oh, it's very noisy here with those men playing dominoes." What these strangers didn't realise was that those men had played that game there all their lives and as far as I was concerned they would continue doing so. If the Good Foodies didn't want to stay, that was quite all right with me. As long as they got what the guide promised – good food – I was happy.

'Dominoes remains very popular here and we still have special dominoes drives at Christmas, with beginners joining in. It's great fun and we set tables up all the way from the front door through my private rooms as well as the bar, and we move my furniture out into the conservatory to make room.'

Another time the furniture had to be moved was in 1986, when the pub flooded, in the wake of Hurricane Charlie, which Margaret recalls in considerable detail:

'My daughter Rowena [Hutchinson] woke me at six in the morning and said: "For goodness sake get up – the water's pouring down the dale!" So I hurriedly dressed, grabbed all the money and deeds and went and stood on the hill nearby. It was already

*The ancient but now endangered pub game of knurr and spell, played by two of the pub's octogenarian regulars; the solid ball is made of holly wood*

too late to try to keep the water out. Luckily we didn't have anything stored in the old cellar as it was already bricked up and disused because it was always full of water from the beck. When it was last used I don't know, but it is a beautiful, vaulted place and we found it by accident when we took the end out of the snug. When it was emptied a single bottle was left in there, so after a great downpour, when the beck comes up, you can sit in the bar and hear this bottle banging around against the walls.'

Today Rowena, whose husband is a retired Arkengarthdale gamekeeper, continues to run a 'tight ship', but leaves plenty of room for traditional games. One of these is quoits, which has been revived on a pitch at the back of the pub, and two teams from the dale now play in a newly formed league.

Much more unusual is the very old outdoor game of knurr and spell, revived locally by octogenarian Red Lion regulars Amos Alderson, William Scott and Jossie Harker (who at the age of eighty climbed the pub's plum trees because he could not bear to see the fruit wasted). The game was once very popular in this old lead-mining area, having been associated with mining nationwide, and no doubt many a pint has been won by the successful exponent. A competitor uses a long, flat-ended club to release a ball from a small trap and then he uses the same club to strike the ball in mid-air in an attempt to hit it further than his opponents have managed. At Langthwaite the men have been using a sprung-metal mechanical trap of the type introduced at the end of the nineteenth century, and their solid balls have been carved from holly, but in some areas they are made from other materials.

The centuries-old Red Lion is now a place where the hiker and tourist may buy handy items such as maps, batteries and books – especially those by Herriot – as well as beer; but it remains a haven of yesteryear where, in Margaret's words, 'The locals can gossip away and share all their troubles and joys. It's just like having friends in every night of the week.'

# A FAMILY RECORD
*Over 300 years of Jelfs at the Boat Inn,*
*Ashleworth, Gloucestershire*

Tradition has it that when King Charles II was in flight from his enemies, after the Battle of Worcester in 1651, a loyal subject called Jelf ferried him to freedom across the River Severn at Ashleworth. In gratitude, the monarch granted to Jelf and his descendants, in perpetuity, the rights to Ashleworth ferry crossing, alongside their old farmhouse-turned-inn. But whether the king also gave his seal of approval to Jelf's selling of ale is unclear. Other records suggest that these privileges may have been given to the Jelfs even earlier, by Prince Edward of March (later King Edward IV) when he was fleeing from his enemies of the House of Lancaster in about 1460. Certainly the family was in the village at that time for one John Jelfes was identified as an Ashleworth leaseholder in 1450. Six of his male descendants were listed as being of military age in 1522, with spellings ranging from Jelffe to Gelfe, whereas the first legible recorded use of the current spelling is in a local church register of 1568. But

*(above) The late landlord and landlady, Edward and Louisa Jelf, relaxing in the garden*

whatever the truth behind the legends, the astonishing fact is that the Jelf family have run the Boat Inn at Ashleworth Quay for at least 350 years and perhaps for well over 500! Against so many odds, tucked away at the end of a little lane leading down to the River Severn and about a mile away from the main part of Ashleworth Village, they have survived from the days when men warred with longbows right through to the age of the atom bomb.

Eighty-two-year-old Miss Irene Jelf still has her hand firmly on the helm of the Boat, where she was born on 1 February 1916; but now she is in partnership with her niece, Mrs Jacqueline Nicholls, who has become the actual licensee, so the family's uniquely long link with the pub is set to continue. Most appropriately for these two delightful landladies, with their rich Gloucestershire accents and welcoming, smiling faces, the name Jelf is said to derive from Joly, an ancient word meaning gay or lively. The irrepressible Irene told me about her experiences there as she mopped the stone floor with a practised hand and attended to other routine chores at the start of yet another day:

'My very first memory is of the sheep being washed off the ferry and being given a good rub in the river to smarten them up for market. But some always swam away so people had to be on hand to recover them. In those days most of our customers worked on farms, but others were connected with the river, which was much busier when it was used to transport all sorts of things. Big boats used to go up and down all the time, carrying stone, wheat and petrol. There was also a big coal business here which was run by my mother's family, the Hopkins. We still have an iron thing on the wall so that people could tie their horses up when they stopped for a drink when taking their drays down for the coal.

*The proprietor of the Boat Inn was responsible for running Ashleworth chain ferry until it was washed away just before World War I*

*Ashleworth Quay (Boat Inn, front right) at a time of severe flooding – probably in 1947*

'Next to the coal wharf there was another pub called the Wheatsheaf, which I think sold only cider until it closed in about 1925. Then it was a private house before being demolished in the 1960s. We too used to make cider – over sixty years ago. We still have the press, which we all had to help push round. It was very hard work.

'Father used to run a chain ferry here, but it was swept away by floods just before World War I and he had no money to replace it, so after that he just ran a little punt up to the 1950s. Then the ferry was discontinued. Anyway, as road and rail transport improved there wasn't so much need for it. Nowadays, apart from fields there's not much to see on the far bank, with the nearest village of Sandhurst some distance away. But we still have the ferry rights and with all the interest in outdoor things such as rambling and birdwatching it might well come into its own again.

'For a long time Father was the only person down here with a boat so he was always helping people when they were marooned, fetching their bread, milk and groceries, or perhaps taking them a beer to cheer them up. And he was in great demand during the last war when the RAF boys from the nearby camp had sessions on our piano and the WAAFS had to be taken back and forth on the punt.

'In a small flood Father used to keep a boat up by the massive stone tithe barn, which is now owned by the National Trust, because this and the church have always attracted a lot of visitors and some of them liked to be rowed down for a pint as a novelty. But if the water was in the pub we didn't want to see anyone!

'We used to get floods every winter, until they built the flood bank in 1981. It's a shame that we can't sit in the courtyard and watch the river like we used to. There was always lots of time to sit and stare in the old days. Any floods now go round the back of the Quay rather than come up the front.

'When I was a girl I thought the floods were marvellous because I didn't go to school. Also, when the meadow floods froze we had a lovely ice rink and I used to go round clinging to my brother, who had a pair of skates. But one thing I never liked about the water was all the bodies of drowned holidaymakers which it brought down from upriver. Over the years we had so many the Boat's shed was known as the mortuary.

'Our worst flood was in 1947, after all that snow melted. We had to climb out the bedroom window into the boat and row right round to the crossroads. Father had to

*Irene catching elvers during her younger days and (right) Edward Jelf on his way home from elver fishing*

feed the chickens perched in the rafters of the outbuilding. Over in the church the water was above the pews and in some of the pub rooms it was 5ft deep. You can still see the mark of the water on that dresser there. I thought I'd go off my head trying to clean up. The white tablecloths in the dresser drawer were all brown, but most sadly we lost a lot of very old documents with details of the pub's history. If we had those now it would be much easier for Jacquie to trace our family tree.

'Many's the time I've had to serve people in my wellington boots and when it's been

*The Boat Inn – hardly changed in hundreds of years*

freezing cold without any fire. But with the bank there we hardly ever get the water in now. The last time was in 1990, when Jacquie had to put her swimming costume on to retrieve the picnic tables which were floating away. But nowadays it's much easier to clean up with modern gadgets such as dehumidifiers. It's funny living in a building when the water's in because you hear all sorts of strange sounds such as the gurgling of empty beer bottles filling up.

'There used to be a tremendous lot of salmon caught here and Dad was always eel fishing to get a bit of extra money. The angling club used to be very large and we always served them out-side. One of them would come in and say, "I'll 'ave sixty pints to start and while you pour those I'll find out what the others want." One old chap who used to come down for the elvers always brought his own bread and bacon, which he'd put on a fork and toast over our fire, making the bar smell wonderful.

'We used to sell a lot of beer in jugs, mostly to card players. I supposed they wanted to concentrate on their game rather than be up and down for pints. When I was young we used the Royal Well Brewery at Malvern and Warn's from Tetbury, before we changed to Stroud. Nowadays it's all different and we always have about four and sometimes as many as nine real ales because we get visitors from all over the place and they like a good variety.'

Today the Boat Inn remains delightfully unspoilt, which is not surprising because when the far-sighted David Jelf left the place to Irene's father, in 1903, he stipulated that there should be no alterations. Of course, there have been some changes, such as the recent creation of a small shop in what used to be the brewhouse, but when you go into the bar it is still like stepping into Miss Jelf's private parlour. If you want to play shove-ha'penny or dominoes, or simply sit quietly and reflect on where Man went wrong, then this is the place to be. And despite the building's great age there is no need to worry about ghosts. Irene insists that the spirits there are very mellow because the Jelfs have always kept their haunt in the family – perhaps even since the day it was built, way back in the mists of time.

# BRITAIN'S OLDEST LANDLADY

## *Mabel Mudge, The Drewe Arms, Devon*

Britain's oldest and longest-serving landlady, the late Mabel Mudge, was a lifetime tee-totaller, and although she served innumerable pints for other folk up to her retirement at the age of ninety-nine, 'Aunt Mabel' – as she was affectionately known to everyone – 'only ever had a drop of lemonade. I can't say I ever smoked much either: 'course, in my young days the girls didn't have much smokes anyway.'

Mabel's record tenure was seventy-five years (of seventy-eight in the trade) at the thatched Drewe Arms at Drewsteignton, on the fringes of Dartmoor, and the pub has remained in a 'time warp' to such an extent that it has been widely hallowed as a shrine of yesteryear. When I visited, there was still no actual serving counter and the relatively new varieties of real ale and draught local cider were poured straight from barrels on racks in a genuine old-fashioned tap room. The plain, ancient furniture still bore the carved initials of long-dead customers, and the nicotined décor remained sympathetically Spartan and genuinely distressed. No noisy jukebox or games machine spoilt the relaxed atmosphere or made conversation difficult. Indeed, first-time visitors there

*'Aunt Mabel' served many thousands of pints during her record-breaking
seventy-five years at the Drewe Arms*

understandably spoke with whispered reverence, as if in a museum. Admittedly tasty
haddock and mushroom bake had been added to the menu of home-made soup and filling ploughman's, and it was even hoped to start a restaurant and re-open bedrooms, but
traditional darts, dominoes, cribbage and chess remained the main entertainment.

Originally built to house the masons building the church, just a closing-time stagger
from the Drewe's front door, and now high on the Campaign For Real Ale's list of most
precious and endangered pubs, the 1646 building is also a kind of 'Mudge memorial',
adorned with innumerable tributes – from appreciative customers, brewers, police and so
on – to the modest lady who preferred the gentle, unplanned evolution of warm hospitality and individualism to the characterless, cold bottom line of company theme-plans.

Already long the focus of media attention, Mabel told me a little about her remarkable life when I visited her in Chagford, in October 1995. Surrounded by cards congrat-
ulating her on her recent 100th birthday, she remained alert and still enjoyed an

occasional trip to the nearby Buller's Arms. However, as with many folk of such a great age, her clearest memories were of her early days:

'I was born at Dunsford, on the edge of Dartmoor, on 4 October 1894, and christened Mabel Louisa Ellis. Dad was a farm worker. My four brothers were all away in the first war, two of them getting killed there. After leaving Dunsford school I went a short way to work at Drewsteignton, where I was supposed to be a parlour maid, but I had to do many other things such as milk the cows and feed the pigs. But they was good ol' days working for the Fulford family.

'In 1916 I married Ernest Mudge in Dunsford Church and we ran the Royal Hotel at Crockernwell for a couple of years. Ern's older brother, Alfred, had run the Druid Arms at Drewsteignton since 1894, but in 1919 he decided that he wanted to go into farming, so Ern took over from him as a tenant of Norman & Pring's City Brewery at Exeter.

'In they days there was very little money in running a country pub, our only regular customers being local farm workers whose wages were very low, but there were also men from the lime quarry before it shut in 1902. Trade was specially bad between the wars, with money generally scarce and keen competition with another pub in the village. You had to support it as best you could, so Ern also ran a carrier's business, and drove a horse and cart to Exeter once or twice a week, whenever anyone wanted a bit of anything or had anything important to do. And horses and traps used to be despatched to Moretonhampstead Station to collect tourists staying at the inn; but now there's no station and no accommodation. Horse transport was also used by the villagers to go to Exeter, Newton Abbot and Okehampton for shopping and other business.'

Ern rented a smallholding of fifty acres and grew corn and hay for his horses and cows, from which he supplied the village with milk. The horses were particularly useful when about four to six at a time were needed to drag huge blocks of granite up the hill for the building of Castle Drogo, designed by Lutyens for millionaire Julius Drewe and now in the hands of the National Trust. Soon after the building was finished Mr Drewe persuaded the brewery to change the pub's name to the Drewe Arms, and when they agreed he gave them a smart new inn sign, complete with his coat of arms, which stands to this day. This was not the first time the pub had changed its name. Before it was the Druid Inn it was called the New Inn, the Old Inn – now a restaurant – having been sited opposite. Ironically, the New Inn was actually older than the Old Inn.

With the carting business as well as the inn to run, Ern relied heavily on Mabel, as she clearly recalled:

'My day started at 6am, when I had to milk eight cows before I could even start looking after the inn's guests and attending to all the other pub duties. With seven bedrooms, we generally had visitors from Easter right through the summer. Many holidaymakers came year after year, some for the salmon fishing on the Teign, which was quite good during much of my time.

'All our food was quite old-fashioned and very plain then, with lots of our own home-reared pork and ham, and we killed a lot of poultry, especially at holiday time. And there was lots of game, too, in they days, with rearing fields, pheasants, partridges and rabbits all about.

'Beer came out from Exeter by horse and cart only once a week, so you had to ask for an extra delivery if something special was on, such as Christmas. All we had then was best bitter and ordinary, but we got through quite a bit of it with lots of thirsty farm staff about in they days. Altogether we had what they called a very comfortable life, and it was all friendly then. But women never went into the tap room before the war.'

After World War II, improved transport and greatly increased leisure time brought many more holidaymakers to Dartmoor, so the number of visitors to the pub grew steadily. But apart from having electricity and mains water installed in the 1940s, the Mudges resisted the tide of change and simply let things be, just as the locals had always liked it.

In the 1960s Norman & Pring sold out to Whitbreads. Many of the newcomers were attracted by a plaque near the door awarded by Egon Ronay in 1965, but when they rushed inside in anticipation of a fancy meal they were confronted by a menu still consisting simply of sandwiches or bread and cheese. What Ronay had valued most was the pub's old world charm and the quality of plain fare.

*Although surrounded by booze for almost a century, Mabel was a lifetime teetotaller*

67

After Ern died in 1951, Mabel held the pub licence alone and continued with the help of friends, her only son having died at the age of six months. Some of her helpers were remarkable in their own right, including Dorothy Fox, who made the pub's sandwiches for over forty years! Such strong village support was vital as Mabel became increasingly frail.

When Mabel announced her retirement in October 1994, the pub had been in the hands of only one generation of the same family for over a century! Not surprisingly, when Whitbread eventually appointed a new tenant, the 550 or so villagers were worried that the pub's unique, unspoilt character would be lost. There were even fears of total closure, which for most locals would have been unthinkable as the view was that the village was the church, the pub and the post office. Happily, the villagers' united front helped persuade the brewers – given the constraints of maintaining the fabric of a listed building – to conserve as much as possible of the Mudge magic, and up to the time of writing the owners had kept their word.

Her godson and the grandson of Alfred Mudge, 73-year-old Henry Scott, who farms locally and has known the pub 'since the cradle', told me:

'When Mabel called time that was it and no more drinks were served. But she was everybody's friend and I don't think she had an enemy in the world. She was particularly fond of little children, and every Wednesday night, right up to the time of her retirement, when the chip van came into the village the youngsters would take their chips into the pub and eat them beside the fire. But she also had a lot of elderly friends, some of whom rallied round to help when Ernest died. On a Sunday I saw as many as six of them in their nineties sat down to dinner there. And every year after she was eighty, when it was Mabel's birthday there was a big celebration with the local hunt meeting at the pub in the morning and Morris dancers in the evening.'

'Aunt Mabel' died just two years after her retirement, at the age of 101; but it will be many years before the people of Drewsteignton forget what an enormous and unique contribution she made to village life.

# RECORD-BREAKING REGULARS

*Les and Bruce Hales of Hertfordshire*

Eighty-nine-year-old Les Hales and his fifty-eight-year-old son Bruce have been regulars at The Chequers, in the delightfully named Hertfordshire village of Barley for seventy-one years and forty years, respectively. Their combined 'service' of 111 years at one pub is a record few folk have equalled – and that's without admitting to any under-age practice!

At the start of his drinking career Les had the choice of eight pubs in the village where he is now proud to be the oldest man, and even 'young' Bruce knew five 'boozers' there, but now there are only two. One of the reasons for this decline is that Barley has lost much of its former importance as a commercial and administrative centre. Another is that mechanisation has done away with the need for an army of thirsty labourers on the land in this prime corn country. Indeed, the quantities of beer once consumed by many of the Hales' drinking pals was prodigious. Les has vivid memories of one man in particular.

'Jack Sapsed – Jack Saps we called 'im – was stockman for farmer Walter Doggett and 'e walked to the Wagon [and Horses] every night. He always stood in the same place in

*Les in his favourite corner at The Chequers, where he has been a customer for over seventy years*

the tap room, at the far left of the bar, an' 'e 'ad a pint glass that thick it weighed as much as one of those three bottles of greengages there, which Susan preserved when we got married in 1940. Incident'ly, she entered those greengages in the last Barley show and was given a special prize. They still look good enough to eat.

'Anyway, every single night Jack Saps would drink eighteen pints of dark mild from that heavy glass. And then 'e used to say to ol' Clarence Stone: "Now Mr Stone, I'll 'ave me road drink" – a large gin and orange. An' when 'e'd finished that 'e always took 'ome a bottle of Guinness in 'is pocket for 'is wife.

'Jack never ever 'ad an 'oliday all the time 'e worked for Walter. Because 'e didn't earn enough to pay for all that beer 'e used to go to 'is boss and ask for money in lieu of time off.

'One night Jack walked straight into the telegraph pole which used to be near the pub, an' laid 'imself right out. An' the very next morning Walter Doggett sent a man up to paint white rings round that telegraph pole, so that Jack could see it more easily on 'is way 'ome. An' apart from when a boar pig rolled 'im over and broke 'is arm, that was the only occasion Jack ever left the village of Barley. Both times they took 'im to Addenbrooke's Hospital for treatment.

'All the time we knew 'im, ol' Jack never wore a pair of shoes, only wellin'tons, even when 'e came up the pub. An' as soon as 'e bought a new pair of wellin'tons 'e got a knife an' cut 'em to let the bunion out on 'is right foot. What a character 'e was. D'y'know, one night 'e got 'ome 'e found 'is wife dead in bed and got in beside 'er: 'e weren't goin' to get no doctor out late at night for no one. So 'e didn't report 'is wife's death till well into next mornin'.

'Another great character was Walt Wills, the farmer, who 'ad an 'orse an' cart an' they reckoned 'e could go from Shafen [Shaftenhoe] End to the Bull 'otel at Royston – over four or five miles – in five minutes. When 'e come back 'is 'orse knew they'd always stop at the Wagon, and it would pull up so sharp Walt sometimes fell out the back, where 'e was so drunk. That 'orse knew the times so well that one day it set off back from Royston without Walt, who was too busy drinkin', so Walt 'ad to run after it and jump on board.'

Les himself claims that he has never tried to keep up with the big drinkers such as Jack Sapsed, and today his consumption is even more moderate – 'just a pint and a couple of Gold Labels, an' perhaps the odd whisky'. It is the company that this farm labourer's son has always valued most. He recalls:

'One time, as soon as you went in the pub people'd 'and you their drink while you

70

waited: they'd push their glasses to you an' say "Cheers". And when your own beer came you'd offer some back, just the same – "Cheers"! Course, you 'ad to wait quite a time for your drink in the ol' days as most places the ol' landlord 'ad to go down in the cellar to draw it off. It was specially bad at The Chequers about forty years ago because the ol' land-lord wouldn't even start to serve you and go down the steps before 'e'd finished 'is game of patience. We always reckoned to put two bob down on the counter, say "I'll 'ave a pint, Stan," and by the time we'd walked up the Wagon an' back 'e'd just be servin' it up!

'Course, beer used to be much cheaper. It 'ad to be as most people were pretty poor. I always remember that Father and 'is mate flailed and dressed out fifteen bushel of beans for just two shillin's. So you 'ad to git what extra you could, such as ha'penny for a spar-ra's egg and penny a rat's tail from the farmer. Even when Bruce first started to come to the pub with me it was still only about 1s 5d for a pint of mild and 1s 10d for a pint of bit-ter, but in my young day it were far less. I used to go in The Chequers, put two shillin's on the counter, order a 2oz round tin of Magpie shag tobacca for 1s 4d, a pint of IPA for 4d, an' git 4d change. The brewers then were Rayment's of Furneux Pelham, before Greene King took 'em over in 1931.

'But we've always 'ad a lot o' fun. There was one ol' bloke at Barley, we pulled his leg and told 'im 'e 'ad the football up, which was run down at The Chequers. Then 'e went and bought lots of pints for people an' 'ad to pay for 'em all: poor chap.'

*This remarkable pub sign at Barley is one of the very few in the country which span a road. Once outside the original Fox and Hounds, the sign was moved to its present position when the old pub burned down in 1950. The 'new' Fox and Hounds (above) was formerly known as the Wagon and Horses, and Les has repainted this sign three times.*

Born on 7 March 1909, Les was one of eight children. After attending the local school he had various jobs in farming, gardening, pleasure grounds, a gold refiner's and painting and decorating, retiring at age sixty-nine. He was called up in 1940 and served on ack-ack defence until 1945.

Over the years, through his work as a decorator, Les came to paint one of the most remarkable pub signs in the country, which he told me about as he, Bruce and I mulled over a pint down at The Chequers:

'The original thatched Fox and Hounds was in Barley high street and on its suspended sign the fox chased the hounds from one side of the road right across to the other: one of only two of its type in the whole country. Anyway, it was made of wood and I painted it three times with white lead paint; an' each time I did it they had to shut the road for safety. When the pub burnt down in 1950 the sign was saved and moved to the Wagon, which was re-named the Fox and Hounds. And that sign's still there.

'My very first memory of The Chequers is from 1917, when it was run by Mr Fuller and they held the annual fair outside. The roundabout was turned by a handle and one chap fell out the swings. The pub were a lot smaller then, a real spit an' sawdust job, an' the front used to be where the back is now, facing onto the old road. The tap room was on yer left and as you walked in there was the half-door to the ol' bottle and jug for the ol' take-away.'

The Chequers was much the same when Bruce first knew it:

'In the lounge bar was just an ol' rickety table and deckchairs, an' the tap room 'ad the ol' settles an' tables where we'd play dominoes. There was a counter but no barrels in the bar – the landlord still went down the cellar to draw the beer. An' in the winter that cellar always used t' flood, an' the landlord 'ad a plank across crates to reach the beer. So 'alf the time y' didn't know whether you was goin' to get water or what in yer beer. An' that was only forty years ago.'

When I asked Les if women were accepted in the local pubs in the old days, he told me: 'They didn't think a lot to it then – it was almost a sin. Everybody used to go t' church. My wife played the organ in Barley church for thirty years and our family always did a lot of bell-ringing.'

'Young' Bruce, too, had close connections with the church, but did not always regard the clergy favourably:

'When everyone come out the church at 12 o'clock it was straight into the Wagon, an' the first one in there was the vicar. He'd walk along the road – still with 'is cassock on – takin' 'is surplice off as 'e went. Every time 'e's the first one up the bar – "Large whisky, please."

'*Now* I'll tell you something. As choirboys, every year after the 'arvest festival we 'ad to deliver the fruit an' veg from the church to the elderly people in the village, by bike. My first job was over to Frank Wisby, and he gave me a shillin' in my hand as a thank you. When I got back the Reverend Gurney said to me: "Did Mr Wisby give you any money?" Well, honest boy as I was, I said, "Yes vicar, he gave me a shillin'." "Well, give it to me

*Dominoes has always been a popular pub game: here the local vicar joins some of his parishioners for a game and a beer in the early 1920s*

then," he said: "that goes to church funds." But 'e went straight up the Wagon an' Horses, put my shillin' over the bar an' bought 'imself a large whisky!

'I'll tell you about someone else who was mean, the landlord of this pub – The Chequers – about 25–30 years ago. You'd come in 'ere an' it was always freezin' cold because the fire was never lit, even though it was laid and even with snow on the ground. So one day I lit it m'self an' 'e went absolutely berserk.

'After talkin' to the lads about it, the followin' Christmas mornin' we all wrapped up a log in Christmas paper, came up 'ere and laid all these parcels – each with a gift tag for the landlord – around the fireplace. That did the trick. No way were we goin' to be cold that day. An' another thing we used to do to keep warm was heat a poker up in the fire – if it was goin' – an' put it in our pints.

'They gener'ly 'ad a fire at the Wagon, but 'alf the time you couldn't see it because the ol' landlady there, Mrs Betteridge, used to put her clothes horse round it, with all 'er smalls an' everythin' in full view!

'Another colourful person was the ol' boy down at the Three Crowns, which used to be shut by light! In those days closin' time was supposed to be ten o'clock, but if we's still in there at nine o'clock, next day we went in there'd be bloody murder. The place was just lit by a candle while we played dominoes, so to get rid of us at nine the landlord took the candlestick up to bed with 'im, so we couldn't see anythin'. An' I reckon 'e always run up those stairs because in the short time it took you to get out the front and look up that same candle would be flickerin' in the bedroom. No way that man wanted us in that pub after nine – 'e even took the dartboard and other games out to get rid of us.

'The next landlord in the Three Crowns was just as odd. Like a lot of 'em in those days, Bill Knighton 'ad another job to make ends meet, and when 'e went out 'e left 'is wife to run the pub. But 'e 'ad to be up at seven each mornin' so 'e always used to go to bed at nine o'clock, reg'lar as clockwork. Up 'e'd go and only give the ol' girl another 'alf hour. Dead on 9.30 we'd 'ear three bangs on the floor, which was the signal for 'er to go up, too. But she was a kind person and used to say to us: "Right, boys, now you carry on without me; an' don't forget, when you serve y'selves, put the money in the till, and when you leave put the latch up." So, sometimes we used to be there till gone 'leven o'clock. An' we never ever cheated 'er. We even washed the glasses up before we went 'ome. Before Mrs Knighton took that pub she used to play the ol' pianer in the cinema during the silent films. In those days the film was always breakin' down and she'd get everythin' thrown at 'er from tomatoes to bottles, an' then she 'ad to run out.'

At the Chequers, Les has used the same corner seat for over thirty years, but admits that nowadays, with more passing trade, he sometimes has to wait for his favourite spot. 'Mind you, there aren't many beats me to it. Me cousin Reg comes over sharp on a Sunday and takes me an' Bruce over just after op'nin' time, spot on five past twelve.'

Apart from this, the remarkable duo now rarely have the opportunity to visit The Chequers together, as Les is unable to walk far and Bruce has recently been disqualified from driving for four years through too much Greene King Abbott. Let us hope that Les is still up for a pint when Bruce gets his licence back in the year 2001, as they try to extend their remarkable record.

# THE PUB WITH NO NAME

## *The White Horse at Prior's Dean, Hampshire*

The isolated White Horse, at sleepy Prior's Dean in east Hampshire, is among the most treasured and remarkable of Britain's country pubs. Dating from 1620 and now popularly known as The Pub with No Name, this one-time mediaeval farmhouse has been the haunt of ghosts, poets and royalty, is almost impossible to find without detailed directions (partly because it has no proper sign) and remains almost totally unspoilt by the surge of society. It has been nominated as one of the best three pubs in the country and is one of only two to have been given the *Good Pub Guide*'s top rating of three stars for fourteen consecutive years.

There have been other pubs purporting anonymity, such as the House Without a Name at Colchester and the What's in a Name at Cambridge. It has been suggested that some of these, including the No Name at Gosport, were thus called so that when customers were asked where they had been all day they could, with some semblance of truth, say, 'Nowhere'. But exactly why and when the White Horse became known as The Pub with No Name is not entirely clear, as explained to me by Jack Eddleston, the man who managed the pub for twenty-three years to April 1996 and, under three

*Jack with his remarkable 1996* Good Pub Guide *award*

separate owners, did so much to protect its timelessness:

'Originally it seems to have become known as The Pub with No Name because it didn't have a proper sign, the original perhaps having been removed by jealous locals when the place was becoming too popular with outsiders. Certainly there wasn't a sign there in 1910, when Edward Thomas wrote his first published poem, 'Up in the Wind', about this very pub. That verse says the old sign often used to be blown down and was finally consigned to the bottom of the pond because it used to creak and keep everybody awake, but we never found one when we cleared the pond out.

'Forty years ago, when I first visited the place as a customer, the owners – Strong's – put a board up, but it disappeared within a few days. Whether it was blown down or pulled down I don't know. So all that remains at the top of the post on the nearby main road is a wrought-iron support framing the passing clouds.

'As the pub is so hard to find, being in the middle of a field and concealed by trees, when Surrey Free Inns bought it (in about 1987) they decided to erect a sign opposite the entrance, so that visitors would know which pot-holed gravel track to take. This, too, had no name board, and was simply a smaller replica of the sign frame on the road. But at first, even this wasn't tolerated by the locals, and within days it was pulled down. The area manager blamed me, but I had nothing to do with it. Then, after a few days with the sign laying in the field, he said that I'd better bring it up again, but when I went down it was gone. Three weeks later, when I took the dog for a walk he started barking at something in the hedge, and there was the sign – thrown out of sight. Gales put it back up in 1997 and there it remains, but still nameless like the one on the road.

'One Sunday lunchtime people kept coming in and saying, "I like your sign", but it was April Fool's Day so I assumed that they were pulling my leg. But in the end so many, including strangers, said the same thing I took my binoculars out and looked down the lane. Sure enough, there was a sign there – it was a Thelwell cartoon of a horse with green wellies on. Some of the local lads had put it up the previous night, even though it had been snowing hard.

'The sign stayed there for a couple of days and then I got the ladders out to take it down. But as I was doing this a *Petersfield Post* reporter happened to drive past. When he discovered what had happened he asked if he could take a photo for his paper. But as he was doing this a bearded old chap on a bike stopped and said: "What are you doin', boy? Don't you ever put a sign up there, 'cos there's a curse on this place and if you ever name it we'll all have bad luck."

'But the pub only became widely known as The Pub with No Name during my time, after I started selling a strong bitter called No Name. At first this Ringwood Brewery beer was sold by three pubs, but when its name was changed we were the only one to continue with it under the No Name label. Hence a lot more folk started to call us The Pub with No Name, meaning the one with No Name bitter.

'Despite all this, a lot of the old locals still only use the name White Horse, and if you went up there and asked them where The Pub with No Name is, they'd say: "Never 'eard of it." '

Clearly the name White Horse was fitting for the pub when it was an old coaching inn. Furthermore, what is now the lounge bar was then a smithy, with every facility to service both coaches and horses, and while the thirsty passengers took refreshment indoors the horses could be changed or quench their thirst at the dew-pond. It was not until the Napoleonic wars that the adjacent road was straightened, to speed up transportation, thus leaving the White Horse in its current odd position in the middle of a field. Traces of the original road past the pub are still visible from the air, as once seen by Jack on a helicopter flight.

In 1830 the pub was one of three in the area which appear to have been set on fire by a local vicar who condemned the demon booze. Although extensively damaged, much of the original White Horse survived – unlike the Anchor, a couple of miles away at Anchor Corner on the A32, which never rose again. The vicar's third victim, the Horse and Groom, was rebuilt, but in later years suffered a second fire and was abandoned.

There have been many other remarkable incidents and strange goings on at The Pub with No Name, some of which Jack Eddleston described to me when I visited him in his retirement flat at Rowlands Castle. But first I wanted to know how a northerner came to run such a remote southern pub. In his broad Lancashire accent, Jack told me:

'I was born near Wigan on 15 June 1927 and Father ran an ironmonger's shop as well as being chief engineer for a coal mine. When my wife and I came south I was a milkman at Petersfield for two years and my second-to-last call was the Harrow at Steep. One Friday when I called there for the money, I asked the landlady, Annie Dodd, if she sold pies. She said: "Haven't you had anything to eat, boy?" "No," I replied. "Well, you sit down there," she said, and she came back out with a big bowl of boiled beef and carrots. And every Friday after that she'd make me sit down and feed me up. Her own drink was the Guinness from the drip tray, which she'd put into a screw-top bottle using a little funnel, and was perfectly all right. Subsequently we became very good friends and if ever she heard me she'd call out: "Is that you, milkie? Come on in and have a chat."

'Then I worked for Plessey's, and in the evenings did some bar work. When we moved to Froxfield I became a regular at the White Horse as well as the Harrow, going there three or four times a week, and when the landlord asked if I was interested in running the place I jumped at the chance. For my first fourteen years I worked for the farmer and cricketer Barry Reed, who was often opening batsman for Hampshire. He sold out to Surrey Free Inns with the undertaking that nothing would be changed, and when Gales took over in 1995 they too said they would keep things much as they were.

'Peter Holloway bought the pub in 1961 and during his eleven years he made just a few changes. The previous licensee was the butcher George Ware, who also owned 213 acres of land around the pub. When rationing was still on he had a hayrick just outside and when you pulled a couple of bales out you could see the space inside where he did his illegal pig slaughtering. He also had a donkey and a deer wandering around the place, in and out of the bar. The deer was supposed to have been a New Forest orphan which George reared, but whether it ended up in the hayrick I don't know.

'Before Ware, a Mrs Plumridge was the tenant of Strong's and in those days one side of the bar was used to store coal, and the inglenook fireplace was the little living room behind the bar. Mrs Plumridge would come out from there through curtains to serve you, and often as not she'd have bare feet where she'd been soaking them in a bowl of water. After she'd drawn your beer she'd go back and put her feet back in soak again.

'Dick Brown, the landlord who was there in the 1890s, is said to haunt the pub. He drowned himself in the water tank outside and they reckon he keeps coming round looking for a towel to dry himself off. He was a big chap and the tank lid was small, so he must have had great difficulty getting in. It was about three days before he was found, and during that time the other people there were drinking the water he lay dead in! In 1986 his daughter Violet wrote in my visitors' book: "I was born here ninety years ago", but unfortunately I didn't get to meet her.'

When I asked Jack if he or any of his customers had seen any ghosts in the pub, he was in no doubt:

'We had quite a few strange happenings there. For example, one evening, after all the customers had gone, I was sitting talking to this lad who worked for me when suddenly he said: "Look at that," and when I did I saw this brass candlestick and ashtray move to the edge of a table and fall off. I said: "The girls have wiped those tables and they're probably still wet." But the lad said: "That can't be the reason because the table slopes the other way!" And to prove it he placed a candlestick in the middle of that table, whereupon it went in the opposite direction to the first one and dropped off.

'Another odd thing, which Peter Holloway and me saw several times, was the public bar door slamming open on a quiet evening when there was no wind at all. The first time I saw this there were only three of us in the bar and we all turned round waiting for someone to come in, but nobody did; and there was a latch on that door!

'Then there was this farm labourer who had a peculiar effect on one of our clocks, which a previous landlord had bought at auction and it was supposed to have come out of Queen Victoria's waiting room at Portsmouth railway station. It had a very nice tick, which was a pleasure to listen to by the fire when it was quiet. Whenever this particular chap stood by it, its glass-fronted door would open up on its own, as smoothly as anything. But if anyone else went to open it they'd have to take a penknife to it where the door was so stiff. I myself saw this mysterious opening several times and we used to joke

*The two bars have a wonderful patina of antiquity*

about it, saying, "Old Dick Brown's here again". After this chap died that clock never opened on its own again.

'We had these narrow stairs with a low overhang and a sharp bend, so you'd never get most modern furniture up there, and one of my dogs, a Cairn terrier, used to bound up and down them quite merrily. But one day it suddenly stopped, its bristles went up and it stared into that corner. I said, "Go on, up you go," a couple of times, but no way would it move. So, jokingly I said: "Oh, it's only Dick Brown. Come on, Dick – out of that corner and let the dog up." And blow me down the dog went straight up. This happened on several later occasions, and every time I had to say, "Come on, Dick, let the dog by," so I started believing it myself.

'Another thing, in about 1993 one of my regulars was stood at the bar when I suddenly saw that he'd gone white. I said: "What's wrong, Bob?" He answered: "Somebody just pushed me." "But there's nobody else in," I said. "I tell you, somebody shoved me and I lurched forward onto the bar," he said again. "Well, I saw you do that," I said, "and that's why I thought you were feeling ill."

'I never really believed in ghosts before those incidents, but I do now a bit. Perhaps some of them have followed me round as our old lodge cottage at Froxfield was haunted, too.'

As well as ghosts, the White Horse has attracted many interesting characters and distinguished customers, some seeking simple refreshment away from the spotlight of high-profile activities such as sport, politics and acting.

'Long before my time, the Earl of Tichborne is supposed to have hidden from Cromwell's men in the old warming oven at the side of the inglenook. But I suppose my most famous customer was Prince Andrew, who started coming here when he stayed with the Neilsons at nearby Woolfield Farm, as he went to Gordonstoun school with their son. He'd come down for the weekend about three times a year during vacations and the Neilsons always brought him to the pub. The first time, they introduced him to my wife and myself and said that from then on would we please simply call him Andy or Andrew, so that people didn't know he was in.

'Andrew continued coming to us till he was twenty-one and he'd never leave without attracting my attention at the door and wishing me merry Christmas or whatever. But he was always teetotal there. The only time I saw him with a hangover was on the day after his twenty-first birthday. I said: "You look rough, Andrew." "I feel rough," he said: "somebody must have laced my tomato juice with vodka last night. What would you drink if you had a hangover, Jack?" "A bottle of White Shield Worthington," I replied, "but that's alcoholic." "I don't care what it is," he said, "as long as it makes me

*The Edward Thomas corner*

feel better." So he had this drink and after about ten minutes he came up to the bar and said: "I feel better now – I think I'll have a toasted sandwich."

'In April 1997 Prince Andrew came down to the Gale's brewery at Horndean, for their 150th anniversary, and he started the Millennium brew going. I was introduced to him as I've been working there as one of the tour guides, and as soon as my old pub was mentioned he remembered the two rocking chairs by the fire.

'I never met the poet Edward Thomas as he was killed in the Army in World War I, but his daughter Myfanwy came to the pub till she was eighty, to join as many as 200 members of the Edward Thomas Fellowship, who come every other year on the first Sunday in March for a walk to commemorate Edward's death. He lived at Froxfield and Steep and the White Horse was one of the pubs he visited while out walking. Now part of the bar is known as the Edward Thomas Corner and has a special plaque, and his nephew presented us with one of his tankards.

'We've also had a lot of visits from campers and the Caravan Club who hold rallies in the adjacent field, but not all of them have realised that there is a pub there. I suppose this is not surprising really as the outside is very plain, apart from baskets of flowers, the only suggestions of a pub being the rough wooden benches and tables. At one time the walls hadn't been painted inside or out for decades. But when Peter Holloway's wife, Margaret, decorated the public bar the locals wouldn't use it. So one night Peter turned the oil lamps and paraffin heaters up till they smoked. Next morning there was an awful mess with everything covered in oily soot. But when it was rubbed down it soon mellowed and the locals started to use the bar again. It has never been decorated since.

'Altogether we had a lot of entertainment through the dew-pond round the back. One freezing Saturday in winter, when we were packed out, this lad said to another customer: "It's a job to park here, isn't it!" "And where did you get in?" asked the regular. "On that big patch of cement just outside," replied the lad. "That's not cement, it's ice!" said the regular, and a group of us rushed outside just in time to prevent the lad's Mini sinking, as the hot engine had started to melt the ice.

'Sometimes people would place bets on who could get through the pond on those scramble motorbikes. But most folk got muddy and wet by accident, including car drivers who reversed to go without de-icing their rear windscreens and slid down the bank.

'But the pond's bone-dry now [1997] because in the gales earlier this year one of the big beech trees blew down and punctured the lining, which is probably the old straw/clay mix. It's as well that didn't happen during the Great Storm of October 1987 because then we lost our electricity for a week and as a result the water pump didn't work. So, every time the toilets needed flushing the girls had to go out to the dew-pond with a bucket and rope.

'As well as walkers and car drivers, the White Horse gets visitors in aeroplanes, hot-air balloons and microlights, as it is the highest pub in Hampshire, at about 750ft, and there is so much open space around. One Tiger Moth pilot flies in regularly for a shandy, but not all of his colleagues have made safe landings. One Sunday five planes, including four Tiger Moths, called in while on a *Daily Mail* sponsored flight to Moscow. But they were quite heavy with extra fuel tanks and one thought he was going to overshoot, so he turned and ran his plane into a barbed wire fence in order to stop. Luckily, all he did was tear the fabric a bit, so we patched him up with plastic sticky tape and soon he was on his way again.

'The Hursley Hambledon Hunt used to meet there sometimes and one day some of their hounds got lost and came back to the pub, so I rang the kennel huntsman. He asked me if I had anywhere to keep them for the night as he'd had a few drinks and daren't risk driving. I told him they were asleep by the bar fire and he assured me that they were very well behaved, so that's where we left them until he came to collect them next day.

'One autumn day a young man was slumped over his beer and close to tears at the bar, so one of the locals said, "What ails you, lad?" The stranger said he'd never be able to hold his head up again. Apparently he was a saboteur and that morning, while driving his car along the lanes at speed, trying to intercept the local hunt, he felt a bump. On investigation he discovered that he'd killed the fox!

'The local beagles used to meet here, too, at about 10am for an 11am start, but it was always a job to get them out the pub. Then one day two members staggered off with bottles of country wines and fell asleep somewhere under a tree. They weren't missed until the evening, when the people who were giving them a lift home came back looking

for them. After that the old girl who was the chairman put her foot down and they discontinued the pub meet.'

But perhaps the most interesting person Jack knew was a member of his staff.

'This chap had been a civil engineer and worked for me full-time for about four years, after he came out the Air Force. He lived in a caravan at the back because there wasn't enough room indoors, but he had his meals with us, and all in all he was an excellent worker.

'One day the drayman delivering the beer came in to me and said: "Your mate's collapsed in the cellar." But when I went down he was already cold and had obviously been dead for some time after just finishing cleaning the beer pipes. So I called the doctor and when he came he told me that the man had had an enlarged heart as well as the worst gout he'd ever seen. There was no way he should have been lifting things like barrels, but the doctor couldn't say anything to me because he was sworn to secrecy. It turned out that this chap – 'Crump' (Gerald) Kerr-Ramsay – was a retired wing commander and had been the chief tunnelling officer in *The Great Escape*. In the famous book about it he is mentioned on just about every other page.

'Anyway, the day after Gerald died two of my elderly regulars, one a retired vice-admiral, came in for their usual lunchtime Bass and were happily drinking away when this lad asked for HSB. But when he tasted it he said: "That's not HSB, it's Bass!" So I tasted it and had to admit he was right. Then I went down the cellar to investigate and found that when Gerald had finished cleaning the pipes he must have coupled them up the wrong way. We always said that it must have been his last laugh on the customers, but what really made me chuckle was the fact that those two fussy old regulars who'd always drunk Bass hadn't said a word. They didn't even realise what had happened.

'Gerald had also made a tunnel for me, so that I could put pipes through to the handpumps in the lounge bar. He really knew what he was doing all right, pointing out to me how the loose soil indicated where the old cellar had once been partly filled in. And he came up exactly where he'd put a mark on the bar floor!'

After Jack's wife died, in 1990, he continued to run the pub alone, but this was considerably more difficult without Margaret's strong support, especially in the kitchen. When Gales took over, Jack was already three years past the usual retirement age, but such was his popularity the brewery were happy for him to carry on to seventy. However, Jack subsequently decided to leave at the age of sixty-nine, to avoid the considerable disruption caused by re-wiring the whole place, moving the living accommodation upstairs and building a new dining room, customers having been assured that this work would have no detrimental effect on the aged atmosphere of the two bar parlours.

Today Jack finds that it is the people, rather than the pub itself, that he misses most, and as he now lives quite a few miles away he cannot simply amble along for a pint. However, he does sometimes take his camper van up there for a night or two, having been given a site there for the rest of his life. There he can listen to the wind or relax in a rocker while supping a glass of No Name, and perhaps even renew his acquaintanceship with a ghost or two.

# SLÀINTE!

*The Toast of Ireland in ... A Town Like Borris*

Whereas so many pubs on the UK mainland are brewery-owned, in the whole of Ireland fewer than a hundred are tied houses. Instead, the overwhelming majority of Irish pubs are owned by families, groups or consortia. This has made it much easier for them to retain their charm and individuality and to remain at the heart of both the family and the country community. As a result, in a typical Irish country pub it is often as easy to buy a bundle of peat blocks as it is to order a glass of stout.

That said, the number of licences in the Irish Republic is currently deemed to be excessive, with almost twice as many pubs per person as on the UK mainland. The Irish authorities are keen to reduce the number of licences through natural wastage, and some areas now make it very difficult to get permission to open a new pub.

Ireland has very few of the quaint 'chocolate-box' pubs which are so common in England. Many are relatively plain and have few obvious signs of antiquity or significant historical interest. But it is the character of mine host and the regular clientele which really make a pub, and the great majority of Irish bars are always warm and vibrant – places where total strangers soon strike up conversation and impromptu traditional music is commonplace.

North and south, no matter where you go in the thirty-two Irish counties, the 'craic' (crack) is inevitably 'mighty' and full of blarney, perhaps typified by the small country town of Borris, in County Carlow. There, in the grand company of my friends the O'Neills, from nearby Muine Bheag (Bagenalstown), I particularly enjoyed visiting several esteemed establishments.

At O'Shea's, in Main Street, proprietor Jim told me: 'Many's the hours I was up in the window as a boy, watchin' for the guards [Gardai, or police], and when I spotted trouble I had to run down and warn everyone.' It was not surprising, then, that O'Shea senior was in court 'only eight times in sixty-three years for allowing after-hours drinking'.

Things have changed a lot since the O'Sheas bought their bar and shop, for just £1,500, in 1934. Jim told me: 'Closing used to be at ten each night, except on Wednesday, when we had a half day, and the guards were very strict. However, you could serve "travellers" to 11pm, meaning people who were living or staying over three miles away. Mind you, even if they only stayed to ten some barely made it the three miles into bed.'

The bar certainly had its characters. Paddy O'Neill particularly remembered Telegraph McCarthy: 'A grand fine feller. When they put the electricity in, durin' the 1940s, he'd carry one of those poles on his shoulder!' No wonder he had a fearsome thirst.

Among the women, Jim recalled Chris Murphy: 'A great old lady who always had a pint of stout and puffed on a clay pipe with most of the shank gone, so she had to hold it right up against her mouth. Course, for most people the thing was with a clay pipe that if you dropped it you never bothered to pick it up as you knew it was broken. In Chris's day, up to the early 1960s, if any other woman had come in the bar it would have been the talk of the county. Mind you, it wasn't easy to hide then because if we had nine people in we were busy, whereas today, with the extension and as many as 200 customers in, we need nine just to serve!'

At that point I paused to quaff my next pint of Guinness. As I eased my way into

(left) (l to r) Paddy, Mary, Declan and June O'Neill enjoy a glass of stout at O'Shea's, a traditional family pub

(right) O'Shea's, Borris, where landlord Jim used to sit in the window looking out for the gardai

the glass, Paddy remarked: 'Look at that – you can see the sips all the way down,' referring to the characteristic creamy marks on the side.

The O'Sheas did not get any draught beer until the 1960s and were still bottling stout about twenty years ago. Jim still has the old corking machine and related apparatus among his wonderful display of artefacts. His Guinness would have been in bottle for ten to twelve days, to condition, before being sold for 1s 9d a pint, which may be compared with £2.20 in 1997. With spirit sales dropping among the increasingly young clientele, Guinness had become the main winter drink at O'Shea's, with Smithwick's bitter the favourite summer refreshment.

Jim O'Shea has been very successful in blending the old and the new, using materials such as an old altar rail and church seating as part of his extension. He might have the very latest Mercedes in the yard, but his bar remains a place of great character, where you can still buy potatoes and a pound of nails within a few feet of the Guinness pump. He never lets things get out of hand, having 'never allowed cards in as it always ends up in an argument'. But then, he should succeed if he abides by the old notice prominently displayed on his bar wall:

---

### TEN COMMANDMENTS OF GOOD BUSINESS

1) A customer is the most important person in any business.
2) A customer is not dependent on us – *we* are dependent on him.
3) A customer is not an interruption of our work. He is the purpose of it.
4) A customer does *us* a favour when he calls – we are not doing him a favour by serving him.
5) A customer is *part* of our business, not an outsider.
6) A customer is not a cold statistic – he is a flesh and blood human being with feelings and emotions like our own.
7) A customer is not someone to argue or match wits with.
8) A customer is one who brings us *his* wants – it is our job to fill those wants.
9) A customer is deserving of the most courteous and attentive treatment we can give him.
10) A customer is the life blood of this and every other business.

---

From O'Shea's we moved along to the cosy Joyce's Bar, but unfortunately I did not get to chat with the proprietor as he was attending to his other duties as an undertaker! However, I did enjoy a good glass of stout there, with my companion and another customer who came down for his regular 'giving out' – talking about all the things that had made him angry that day.

At Dalton's Bar, another very friendly landlord called Jim told us that he, too, had been there all his life. 'I couldn't be here any longer, could I?' he added with an impish grin. In fact the pub had been in the Dalton family since the days of his great-grandfather, but Jim had no idea how old the building was. The bar continues to double as a shop, and also

---

*(right) Dalton's bar and shop, one of thousands of small Irish pubs at the heart of the country community*

offers a hairdressing service, as I was surprised to discover when I opened the wrong door in quest for the loo!

Dalton's Bar, too, once had old Chris Murphy as a customer. Jim told me: 'She was usually called Mrs Chris, after her husband, which was a common practice in Ireland. The chalk [clay] pipes she smoked were made at Knockcroghery, in County Roscommon, and we'd receive them in a big box full of sawdust. Up to about thirty or forty years ago we gave them away with tobacco and some people broke off a piece of stem immediately.'

Of course, not all customers were as passive as Chris Murphy, as Jim remembers only too well:

'On the old monthly fair days there'd generally be a few arguments and fights over anything at all, such as the lads from each area settling old scores over hurling, or the heavy gambling that has always been common in pubs. You never knew what to expect. About twenty years ago a chap even brought a calf in the bar to sell it to another customer. But now the fair is only annual.

'I was attacked once, on 14 August – the day before the big fair. These young tinkers were trying to drive their car through my hall door, so I went out and took a swing at one, but he knocked me right out. They were angry at not being able to get a drink, but in those days it was common for landlords to close their doors to troublesome tinkers and only let the locals in.

'The problem was you could never get the guards over quickly to help, so you had to look after yourself. Some of them were fearful anti-pub and with the after-hours raids they'd put a man at the back while others came in the front. And if they suspected that a customer didn't qualify for the extra hour they'd soon get out their special chain (22-yard measure) and actually check the distance. It wasn't so much where you lived but where you slept the night before.'

Like the O'Sheas, Jim Dalton bottled his own Guinness and Smithwick's up to about twenty years ago. The whiskey was delivered in barrels, and the Daltons once had a hydrometer to test it so that they knew how much water should be added to give the right strength. Later, of course, branded whiskey was of guaranteed strength.

Paddy O'Neill's great friend and neighbour at Muine Bheag, octogenarian farmer Dan Maher, knew both these bars plus quite a few others, such as the Railway Inn, where the landlady was a

*At Dalton's bar whiskey used to come in barrels and gallon jars, and water was added to adjust the strength*

*Jim Dalton, still smiling after a lifetime behind the bar once run by his great-grandfather*

chiropodist and cut customers' toenails in between serving stout. Another of Dan's haunts in Main Street, Borris, was Hickson's, now the Corner Bar, where 'they used to have straw and sawdust on the floor and one man had a tame fox which stayed wrapped around his neck while he had a pint'. He also vividly remembers one particular time he went in there with Sonny Fenlon: 'Sonny was very drunk so the landlord said to me: "I'll serve you but not him." Sonny shouted at him: "You Kerry bastard," but he had a few [drinks] on him all right and caught his head in the bat-wing [swing] doors as he staggered out!'

Dan himself was quite a wild one in his day and drove around in 'a big maroon Jag bought from Paddy Byrne when he was had up for speeding. He told me: 'Once I was coming back from Dennison's and I think I must have fell asleep because the car went off the bridge. And another time I went through Roly Kidd's wall. But then the guards didn't care a damn about drinking and driving. Once we went in the Hunter's Rest on the way back from coursing in Fenagh and the guard was so merry he was knocking sparks off the floor' (dancing with his hobnail boots on) 'and Sergeant Grey would drink a lot of whiskey while playing poker with hundreds of pounds on the table.'

# MAID OF THE MOUNTAINS

## *Marie Osborne of Rathanna, County Carlow*

Within the shadow of Mount Leinster, the highest peak in the Blackstairs range and the second highest in Ireland, lies the remote little village of Rathanna, where Miss Marie Osborne continues to run a business that has remained remarkably unchanged since she was born there on 22 July 1926. The combined bar and shop, which had been bought by Marie's parents, is still without running water, and there is not even a toilet – of any description – where desperate customers may find relief. Even inconvenienced ladies are obliged to make use of the handily adjacent 'waste' ground, where cottages once stood, hoping that no eyes are peering from nearby windows.

Octogenarian Dan Maher remembered how, not that many years ago, 'Osborne's always had a candle in the bottle and you couldn't see what you were drinking'. Today, although the bar now has electricity, you might still struggle to see there because Marie appears to be half owl. When we visited her in the afternoon she did not switch the light on until dusk could not get deeper, and for a while I literally could not see to write in a room which is gloomy anyway, even at midday. Ironically, as the light faded, I could just see light bulbs among the many and varied items for sale behind the bar! It seemed as if Marie was in mourning for her two old Tilley lamps, and she admitted: 'I miss them great because they kept you warm as well, although you couldn't light 'em up in a hurry.'

The fact that Marie has continued to run the bar alone since her brother died is a tribute to her great bravery and determination, for in the five years from 1991 to 1996 this softly spoken lady suffered three frightening burglaries and one attempted burglary. It was not surprising that we were greeted by a very suspicious German shepherd dog called Boxer. Indeed, John Byrne, the kind local man who gave us a lift there, would not even get out of his car because he was afraid of that dog. Furthermore, Marie had recently installed a modern electronic alarm and put bars across the windows, and confided that she had also just bought a shotgun and 'hoped to get a licence'! However, it was 'only a single-barrel model' as she did 'not expect to kill anyone, only make a noise and frighten them off'.

Considering how badly she herself has been frightened, I would not have blamed Marie if she had adopted a much tougher line. Not only has she been woken to find balaclava-wearing burglars beside her bed, but also she was once beaten up by one, who turned out to be a local lad aged only fifteen.

On one occasion Marie had a handbag full of bills hanging on her bed and the thieves took this, assuming that it was stuffed with cash. When they ran outside to their car, Marie chased them and fell, hitting her head on a door.

In January 1996, at 3am, three intruders broke into Marie's bedroom and demanded money. When she told them that there wasn't any, one of the thugs whispered that he would kill her and then threatened to set the house alight. She tried to reason with the man by asking how he would react if his mother were robbed in this way, and then the brutes left, but not before blocking her path with a dresser. Next day all she noticed missing was an oil heater from the shop.

The nearest gardai station is five miles away, at Borris, but on each occasion Marie failed to get a response to calls there 'because you can't get them after half five in the evening', so she now rings 999 if she requires assistance. No wonder that she no longer sleeps very well but wakes at 2am every night and says to herself, 'I'm not safe until four'.

On top of all this trauma, Marie's property has been severely damaged by fire:

'We were late going to bed and my brother Harold fell asleep in the kitchen as he was so tired. At three o'clock he woke and said to himself, I'd better go to bed now and see that everything's secure before I go.

'At four o'clock I awoke and saw smoke in my room, so I went to tell Harold. "Ah," he said, "there's no smoke in my room – there's nothing wrong." But luckily he did get up to help me check. I went down into the hall and there was no smoke there at the time, but the next thing the whole bathroom came crashing down into the kitchen at the back. So I said, "That's it – there's no way we're staying in this place tonight", but before we went out the door from the kitchen to the hall went up in a ball of flames. Then the stairs went.

'Unfortunately, the firemen were too far away to come quickly, but when they did arrive we got two brigades! They managed to save this bar, except for the patch of wooden ceiling panels which have been replaced in the corner, as well as the store next to it, but the whole of the back of the building was destroyed and it cost me a fortune to have it renewed. Sadly, all our old photos and papers were lost in the blaze. We didn't discover the cause of the fire but I reckon 'twas the butt of a cigarette.'

Fortunately, the fire did not reach Marie's 40-year-old petrol pump, close to the front of the building near the hitching rings where customers' horses used to be tied to the wall. In the old days Marie sold Shamrock petrol and from her one pump she now sells only four-star. She has 'thought about changing to the unleaded' but does not want to let the regulars down as most of them have old cars which haven't gone green'. Her petrol trade remains quite good, because even with new outlets her nearest competitor is over five miles away.

Marie paused to make us another of her excellent hot whiskeys, just the way I like them with plenty of cloves but sparing on the sugar. To prepare this popular tipple she used a most surprising aid. How strange it was to watch our glasses revolve in a counter-top microwave until we could see their delicious contents gently bubbling by the only light within that dark room. It was a most striking contrast between old and new.

Marie had a good education at boarding school, but she returned to the pub at age fourteen and has been there ever since.

'We used to have many more regular customers because there were a lot more houses round here and they were all occupied by big families. But gradually lots of them emigrated to America or wherever and families died out, so the buildings were neglected. Now people come here and wonder how anyone could ever have lived up there on the bleak mountain.

*Marie has sold petrol for many years*

'You see those hooks up there above the counter? That's where we had some copper scales which you pulled down to weigh the tobacca, which we cut with a knife from a big slab of twist. Sometimes you wouldn't be that smart and get the exact ounce, so then you'd have to put on a jockey [smaller piece] from the tat. And when you'd done you put the scales up again out of the way.

'We also sold the ling fish, sides of bacon and – up to about thirty years ago – pigs' heads which Father bought by the ton from Buttles of Enniscorthy. Every man up the road here would go home with a whole head or two after enjoying his drink. There were tongues in those heads, too, and there'd be plenty of meat on them. All the local people were great for growin' their own vegetables, the cabbage, turnips and potatoes – the leek an' all – and these would be cooked up with the pigs' heads to feed a big family.

'Then one day this man, who used to come across the field here to drink and shop, said to my Father, "Why don't you get the pigs' feet, too? They're the greatest thing of all time." So Father got in a hundred and I thought I'd give them a try. But they took hours to cook, and when they were done I could see no meat on them and they were too salty. So we left the rest out in a tea chest in the store, before Father said to go and give them to the two dogs. But when I took them out into the yard each dog picked one up, chewed for a minute and then let it down again. Straight away they were away to the trough, and they were so dry their thirst couldn't be fixed up, the feet were that salty.

'We used to keep pigs ourselves, and every so often we'd go up with the lorry, to Paul Vincent at Dublin, to get a load of meal and other stuff for the pub. Now everythin's delivered, most pig keeping's gone out and fewer people keep cattle on a small scale. But I still fatten a dozen or so, which I look after myself on my thirty-four acres.'

Among Marie's customers have been quite a few with colourful names, such as the inexplicably named Paddy the Rock and John the Gap, two men from Tomduff 'who were very good at stretchin' the trut', and the comedians on TV wouldn't be a patch on them'.

'We used to have a lot of fun together, with me playing the piano, but that got burnt in the fire. Also, my brother was a fine singer and good at pickin' up tunes on the accordion. He'd often get everybody going, but nowadays they need more tuning with drinks before they start up. A few still come in and play the squeezebox.

'We've always opened seven days a week, but not all day. I'm usually open now from ten in the morning to twelve in the night, with people coming from all over, from Myshall and Kilteavy and all sorts of places as they move around more now. The trouble is nowadays a lot of the lads don't come in the pub till gone 11pm and often keep me up well into the night, and when they get the habit that's it! But you've got to do it as a lot of the pubs are at it now.

'Another thing is the trade's been hit by the drunken driving, and now they're after you for the speedin', too. But it's incredible what some people can drink and still drive all right. There's a fellow comes in here from Wicklow way: well, the first time he came he was already well "up", and then he had a few more so he must have been very drunk. He had a huge car by the door and when he went to go I thought he'd have the wall down. But he turned without makin' a single mistake, and he always gets home all right, too.

'Nobody comes on their bike now – it's all cars. A couple of years ago the bikes came back a bit when people started getting interested in the exercise, but that didn't last long when they found out what hard work it was on the steep roads round here. It must be twenty years or more since many people came to shop and drink here by horse and cart, but some continued after that, even on horseback.'

I asked Marie how the popularity of various drinks had changed and she told me that she now sells more stout – mainly Guinness – than anything else. When I enquired as to how much of this was bottled I was amazed at her reply: 'All of it, though I hear it's a coming thing the draught. But I won't ever have it because when the bar's full up it would take me ages to let all the glasses of draught settle before I could top them up, and people are very particular with their pints. Also, with the bottles you can keep on with the same glass all night, so there's less washing up.

'We used to buy whiskey by the gallon and bottle it up. One old fella from Wexford started callin' a few years ago, to try to get me to buy the poteen – but I never took it because I couldn't sell it. He last came in only a few months ago and said: "Go on, buy a bottle, because I haven't the price of a smoke and that's the only way I can buy a packet of cigarettes off you." So I said: "I won't, and that's that!" "Oh, give me ten cigarettes," he said, "and I'll pay you next time I'm up this way." But I didn't give in.

'There was a lot of borrowing in the old days, but now I only give credit to a few people I know well. There's one farmer with an account for his petrol and drinks, but he's very reliable, and there's a few more who pay me every week. Sometimes I still get strangers in from lower Wexford, or wherever, and they say would you lend me a tenner, but I always say "No, I'm not a money lender!" '

Being opposite the church is a distinct advantage for the pub, as Marie explained:

*The village pub in the forties: a place to relax after a hard day's work*

'They have mass here at half nine and then a lot of the people come over here at half ten. Some want a few groceries or the weekly papers but more want a drink – a glass of stout or a half one [single whiskey] to warm them up. We have the two priests in, too. They come out from Borris now as they have several places to look after. One has the brandy, the other the whiskey, and when they have relatives comin' they always bring them over to see me.

'I still buy all my regulars a drink at Christmas, but Christmas Day itself is the only day I shut. Mind you, I still have to warn the people that I won't open because they used to come knocking at the windows and I had to tell them to go away. December 25 is when I visit my friends at Gorey, on the Wexford coast, but it's a very long day for me because I have to feed me cattle before I go and I'm away for me dinner and supper, before returning that night. My friend comes to collect me and brings me back, but I have to lock the dog in because she's frightened out of her life by him and won't let him in her car.

'Other than that I hardly ever go anywhere. But all of us publicans in the area once had a good outing to the Guinness brewery in Dublin. They gave us a free drink before lunch, then we toured the brewery and had our photos taken, and then we had a few hours to do our shopping. It was great fun and everyone was singin' on the way back.

'I don't do anything special on New Year's Eve, but I may have as many as thirty people in. They like to go over and ring the bell at midnight, but once the rope broke and this poor ol' feller fell down on his back, so now they have a chain. Generally they're a good crowd now and there's no snobbery, but in the old days I had to put one or two farmers right when they turned their backs on the very poor ones. I haven't had to throw many people out over the years, and even when I did they'd be back the next day and there'd be no hard feelings about it. And I don't see many tinkers now because that dog's good at keeping 'em away. Not that they're really bad people but they'd always be round tryin' to buy your furniture or sell you somethin', an' all that.'

Despite having had more than her fair share of trouble, Marie would run a pub if she had her time over again. Furthermore, she conceded: 'I'd rather live now than in the old days. I can't imagine how we managed without electricity. But I do miss my old range, the big crane in the open fireplace to hang pots on, and that wonderful smell of smoke right through the pub. Course, we were lucky in having loads of sticks out on the land. Now I just have this modern cooker but you can't sit down to it because there's no fire to look at.'

When we said goodbye to the delightful Marie I felt so sad that she had no close family to carry on the business which dominated *her* life and still bore the name of her father: T. Osborne. Her closest relatives were nieces, but I doubted whether their generation would have the resilience and wonderfully dry sense of humour to carry on as she has done. When the maid of the mountains finally calls time, Rathanna will never be the same.

# KEEPING THE PEACE

*Marjorie Hardacre of Somerset and Wiltshire*

It was in the light of considerable first-hand experience that 77-year-old Marjorie Hardacre (née Southway) told me: 'When the drink's in, the wit's out,' for in some sixty years service behind the bar she has witnessed many volatile situations. Indeed, one was literally explosive and happened right where I was sitting when Marj told me about it at the Crown Inn, Pilton, near Shepton Mallet:

'One of the farmers put some gunpowder in the ash tray on his table and sat round with his friends till *wooomph!* – someone put a lighted cigarette in it. The result was obviously much more violent than the farmer had expected. The fluorescent light on the ceiling shattered, one man had a hole blown through the rim of his trilby and another was so startled he sat with his mouth wide open for over half an hour. Mum and Dad had been sleeping upstairs and came running down to me in a panic, and not only was I completely stunned but couldn't hear for two days.'

But that prankster hadn't meant any real harm, any more than the drunk who once

*(above) Christmas Eve festivities, with Marj (left), Jack Cox and the 'gleanie', and 'Little Billy'*

*The Crown Inn as Ken and Marj Hardacre (centre) first knew it in 1950*

poured Guinness all over Marj for no reason at all. However, there were many times when Marj really did need to run for help.

'When I was ten, in 1931, Father became tenant of the Railway Inn at Wincanton, and that could be a very rough place. Lots of tramps came in as they had a lodging house along the road, but they always had to go in the special room Dad provided for them. When they were drunk, and he told them they weren't having any more, they'd throw their glasses in the fire or even through the window. I should like as many pints as times I had to run for the police there.'

Marj started serving at the Railway Inn (now demolished) when she was only twelve, when her mother went into hospital. This was a daunting job for a girl, as no women customers at all went in that pub until the outbreak of war in 1939, and it was also in a very basic environment:

'There was sawdust on the floor and spittoons which Father emptied and blackleaded every day. But it was always filthy, of course, as lots of men used to chew tobacco.

'Livestock were auctioned close by, so on market days, when we were extra busy, Dad kept the swing door in the passage open to make access easier. One day a cow got away from a drover, came in that door and got stuck. There was no way it could turn round so the drover got a mallet and pushed the animal forwards – all through our back room and beer cellar, until it was free.

'With the cattle market opposite we did a lot of food there and we were open from 10am to 10pm, but there was only one little bar. The rest of the pub was just rooms where the farmers would sit around with their drinks, and I had to take them their bread and cheese, for which Dad used to give me a penny for sweets.'

When war broke out, eighteen-year-old Marj remained at Wincanton to work as a book-keeper for seven years, while her parents moved to Market Lavington, Wiltshire, where her father became tenant of the King's Arms. After the war, Marj went to help her parents at the King's Arms, but times were still very difficult.

'We could open whenever we wanted to within the legal hours, but with the rationing still on there was only enough drink for us to open three days a week – usually Wednesday to Friday. We'd put up notices saying open at eight in the evening, and you should have seen the tremendous queues that formed!

'But one person who didn't go without his booze was the butcher. He always came down at eight in the morning and had his two double Scotches – and then we'd be sure to get the meat we wanted!'

When Marj married Ken in 1946, she went back to live at Evercreech (some three miles from Pilton), the village in which she had been born on 12 August 1921. There she and her husband lived with her mother-in-law for 3½ years, before fate took her back into pubs.

'My husband came home and told me the Crown was going, but I didn't really want a pub as you couldn't get any time off – my parents hadn't ever had a holiday! But in the end I agreed, and in 1950 we moved into the Crown as tenants of the Charlton Brewery, later George's, then Courages and now Ushers.

*Marj's parents, Jessie and Lilly Southway, behind the bar at The King's Arms, Market Lavington*

'It was very different with the old breweries, when it was less big business. Then it was always Mr and Mrs Hardacre, but now you're just a number. Also, they actually used to come and collect the rent and always left half a crown for us to have a drink on them.

'We used to get through a lot of rough cider at the Crown – sixty gallons a week from a local farm. And back at the Railway, Dad used to keep ginger to sprinkle on it. We still have some of the old cider cups here, one printed with "Crown Hotel, Pilton", and one or two are still used. And that conical copper container hanging up from the beams is what they used to warm the cider in.

'And there's been quite a few years when our customers really did need warming up, such as in 1963. That year, to get the beer, my husband had to borrow a Land Rover from a farmer and drive into Shepton on top of the hedges – the snow was so deep and frozen hard. And we were extra busy because so many local people couldn't get to work and just sat around drinking.'

Marj has also had a great deal of fun at the Crown. For example, one Christmas Eve Jack Cox decided to pluck a gleanie (guinea fowl) in the bar, just for a laugh, and when Marj came down on Christmas Day 'there were feathers everywhere'. Then there was the customer who, without asking, brought his horse into the bar to make a point to a friend, as if it were something you did every day.

The inn and the easy going way of life had changed relatively little since Fred and Alice Harvey ran it from 1908 to 1919, and made their own cider there. During their tenure Pilton boasted its own brewery as well as seven pubs, but when the Hardacres moved in, the Crown was the only pub left in the village. The Harveys continued in the cottage opposite, where Fred had been born in 1873, but by then Fred had become very wary of the greatly increased traffic, so Marj used to 'see him over the road to the pub at twelve o'clock and back again at one'. Today he would be even more concerned. 'So many more lorries now thunder through the village, especially since the tolls over the Severn Bridge have become so expensive and drivers look for alternative routes.'

Ken Hardacre died in 1988 and in 1989 Marj's son-in-law, Tony Sherwood, became the new licensee, ably partnered by Marj's only daughter, Pauline. Today, with a skittle alley where the old coach house and stables used to be, the sixteenth-century inn continues to thrive and the youthful Marj remains as busy as ever, pulling pints.

*(above) The Crown in 1963, when Marj's father had to drive along the tops of frozen hedges to collect the beer
(right) Marj and Ken with Mr and Mrs Harvey, who kept the Crown from 1908 to 1919*

# GOING OUT
# IN A BLAZE OF GLORY

*Pam Harvey-Richards of Dorset and Hampshire*

Being a third-generation publican and having spent half a century living in pubs, Pam Harvey-Richards was feeling very sad at being forced to leave the trade at the age of fifty-nine, following the death of her second husband. As Pam told me, 'The brewery just didn't want old women as licensees any more.' So, to cheer herself up on her very last day as mine host, in chilly autumn, Pam said to her daughters: 'Let's show everyone what a good fire really should be like.' But then things became rather overheated, as Pam remembered with mixed feelings as we sat in the pub in question – the appropriately named Green Dragon, in the New Forest village of Brook.

'In the Forest some properties have the ancient common of estovers, which is the right to cordwood, so it was easy for us to get 4ft logs for the fire. With a pair of fire dogs in the hearth, we simply pushed the ends in as the log burnt. Once going, the fire was kept in all winter, so all we had to do was clear some of the ash each morning.

'On this particular day we got this red-hot fire going quite early, but it wasn't long before someone came in and said there's smoke coming out of the roof. So we rushed outside and I was horrified to see that the thatch had caught fire. I phoned the Fire Brigade and six fire engines came out very quickly indeed because it was a thatched roof and we were having a dry time. They soaked the whole roof, put the hose down the chimney and soon had the fire under control. Luckily, nothing downstairs was burnt but everything, including the bar, was black with smoke. But then lots of customers and all the people working for me rallied round, took everything down for washing and cleaning, and that afternoon you wouldn't have known there'd been a fire there. So that evening we were able to open as planned and about five or six hundred people – all my

friends – came to say cheerio. We all did the hokey-cokey up the road to the Bell Hotel, into the gents' toilet there and back again. And that night they presented me with a wonderful green dragon mounted on a plinth.'

An only child, born at Upper Parkstone, near Bournemouth, on 18 February 1925, Pam also had an exciting time after her father took the St Leonard's Hotel, between Ringwood and Ferndown, in 1936.

'The St Leonard's was brand-new and more of a road-house on the A31, so we were one of the first to target travellers with snack food. However, it was very rural there then, with only a few houses nearby, and we had a

*Ex-landlady Pam Harvey-Richards*

very large garden and two or three acres of forestry land as well as nearly an acre of gravel in front of the pub. Until about three weeks before the opening date, the surveyor hadn't realised that there was no electricity in the area, but Father was friendly with the MD of the Bournemouth Gas and Water Company and persuaded him to put in the very latest in gas appliances, including floodlights outside and wall lights in the bar. They gave lovely soft lighting, and during the war it was wonderful because we could still see on the many occasions when most other people had their electricity turned off. Also, where people were short of fuel they used to come in the pub and stand under the lights to get warm. We had coal and wood fires as well, but you couldn't use as much solid fuel as you'd like.

'The public bar had lino on the floor because all the workmen came in there, but the lounge had carpet, and in the middle was an off-sales where the old ladies used to come for their bottle of gin or cider. Our beer, from Strong's of Romsey, included a fairly weak mild called SAK, a stronger mild called 3X, and PA bitter, at 3d, 4d and 5d per half pint. Woodbines were tuppence ha'penny for five in paper packets.

'During the war my father was also in charge of the underground for the area from Bournemouth to Portsmouth and we had an underground transmitting and receiving radio station in the pub grounds. I can remember when it was dug out. It was a great long place with a tunnel leading to a ladder and a trap door with a little tree stump on top for camouflage. There were lots of pine trees and heather around it in our garden, and when I was home from boarding school one of my jobs was to throw pine needles,

*The Old Fox in Bournemouth around 1890*

which I kept in a sack, over the cracks around the trap door whenever someone went through it. Also, along the pathway between us and the next property, there was a bell push behind a bit of bark on one of the big trees, and if anyone approached you lifted the bark and pressed the button to warn the people down below not to come up. It was all very secret.

'Radio messages were received from the Continent and translated there, using a code which changed every eleven hours. Much of the translation was done by an army officer called Betty, who worked behind our bar as a cover, she and my father doing four hours on and four hours off. But once she didn't come up on time, so Father went down to investigate and found that Betty had been overcome by fumes from a smoking oil lamp. She'd got to the bottom of the steps but couldn't manage to climb them. Thankfully they got her out just in time.

'We used to get lots of pilots in the pub, especially from Ibsley, including famous ones such as Guy Gibson and Johnny Johnson, who were household names at the time. And we all had some great times together. I'll never forget VE day in 1945, when a squadron of New Zealanders danced the harka in the pub. They were great big blokes – three of them Maoris and four half-Maoris – and they stamped about so much that the floor joists dropped.

'Another time these RAF chaps came in from Stoney Cross and said to Mother: "Oh Dorrie, it's your birthday; look what we've bought for you," and they gave her a large rhododendron in half a beer barrel. Also, one of them had an army hat with gold braid all over it. Well, they hadn't been there long when the phone went and it was our good friend who ran the Royal Bath Hotel at Bournemouth. "Have those RAF chaps come into you, Ted?" she asked Father. "Yes," he said, "are you missing something?" "Yes," she replied, "the brigadier says that unless he gets his hat back he's not going to pay my bill; and they've taken one of my rhododendrons". So Father said: "Well, the rhododendron's here and you can have that back, but I don't know about the hat," whereupon all the chaps in the bar disappeared and went back to Stoney Cross, where they threw the hat under some gravel being tipped off a lorry!'

In 1951 Pam married and lived in regimental quarters. When her husband left her, she returned to the St Leonard's for a further eight years before marrying again. She helped her second husband run a wholesale newspaper business until one day in 1963, when she was out delivering papers in deep snow and 'couldn't stand it any more'. So they took the opportunity to return to the pub trade. 'At least the people come to you, and they pay cash!'

The couple took the Walkford Hotel, near Highcliffe. At the time, her father's mother, who had run several pubs, told her: 'Remember, always keep your beer bright and your lavatories clean and you'll be all right. And never introduce anybody to somebody else by name.' 'But why?' asked Pam. 'Because you don't know who they're in with,' said grandmother.

'In the old days,' Pam explained, 'it was always the habit of the publican never to speak names but just say something like, "Hallo, my dear". I broke the rule once and always regretted it because this couple were not man and wife and had been meeting privately. They had been regular customers, but after I said the wrong thing they didn't come in again. Oh yes, you have to have a skin like a rhino and let things slide off you in the pub business.'

Drunks, too, need sensitive treatment, but you cannot always steer them in the right direction. 'There was an old girl called Gran, who did our cleaning at the Walkford. Her husband, Harold, was a bit slow and often came in for a drink or two. But one Christmas he kept on being topped up with beer and became very belligerent, so I said to Gran: "You'd better take Harold home – I think he could do with a rest." So off they went. But almost immediately I heard this almighty thud, and when I dashed outside there was poor old Harold cursing and swearing. He'd walked into this cast-iron lamp-post and broken his nose on it. So then, in his drunken stupor, he said to the lamp-post: "OK – you wanna fight, I'll give you a bloody fight." Then he thumped the lamp-post and broke his hand, too!'

Pam and her husband moved to the Green Dragon in 1966, but she had known the pub since the late 1940s, when she met with friends and associates there to buy ponies. Subsequently, Pam's interest in both ponies and the Forest developed to such an extent she went on to hold many related positions, including vice-chairman of the New Forest Association, council member of the National Pony Society, council member of the New Forest Pony and Cattle-breeding Society, judge for most native pony panels, chairman of the New Forest Pony Enthusiasts, member of the breeds committee of the Royal Show, and – in 1997 – president of the New Forest and Hampshire County Show. But when Pam's husband was ill she had to rein back temporarily as the pub trade began to suffer. As Pam said, 'Like you or hate you, what the regulars like to see is the landlord and landlady behind the bar, so that they feel they are being well looked after.'

The customers also like to be welcomed and entertained by a colourful mine host, but not many expect to see animals as a sideshow, as was often the case in the old days at the Green Dragon, as Pam recalled:

'On New Year's Eve I used to bring this stallion in for a bit of fun and he would walk up and down behind the bar. He really liked people and they would give him drops of beer out their glasses, and once he wore a straw hat with his ears sticking out. So old Billy Whitcher, the gypsy, said, "Well, if he's in here I'm bringing my mare Priory

Petunia in," which he did, into the public bar where she couldn't do much harm on the brick floor.

'But the Forest ponies can be a problem for pubs. They've always stood just out here by the pub door, "shading", because they get a nice breeze there when the weather's hot. We often had to tell customers not to touch these ponies because they're wild, but some thought they knew better and ignored us.

'Once I had a goat that walked around the bar. I had to bring up a foal as an orphan, and the cheapest way to do that was on goat's milk, lime water and rosehip syrup. I started with it at the Walkford and we brought the goat with us here to the Green Dragon.

'I also had a pair of Muscovy ducks, and when the female laid an egg my elder daughter, Jocelyn, decided that she was going to hatch it out. Jocelyn was about

(left) *Life is complicated: Pam trying to concentrate on serving behind the bar, while also helping to supervise the loading of a consignment of New Forest ponies bound for France*

fifteen at the time and kept the egg under her jumper until the chick popped out. She would put it on the counter and it would walk up and down and drink water out of the ash trays. And it followed customers around the bar because it thought it was a person. At first we called it Albert, but it turned out to be Albertine. Then Jocelyn felt sorry for her and got her a drake, and after that it didn't want to know humans at all.

'Later on a fox broke into our pen and killed both ducks and all the bantams. I've never liked foxes and I've hunted nearly all my life. When I was at the St Leonard's I used to go out with the Portman, and here at the Green Dragon both the buckhounds and the foxhounds used to meet. But it was one of those controversial subjects which I never discussed in the pub, like religion and politics. If you did you were bound to upset someone.

'At the Walkford I used to do rabbit pies because they were a bit different and people would come for miles to eat them. I bred these large white rabbits in a big shed with wire netting going into the ground all round so that nothing could dig underneath. Unfortunately, one night a fox got in there and killed all thirty or so of my rabbits, as well as about six of my rather nice chickens. The only thing spared was Jocelyn's guinea-pig, because in all the commotion the enamel wash basin had been turned over on top of it. When I went in there the carnage was awful, and the fox hadn't eaten a single thing – just killed the lot and disappeared. I couldn't even use the killed animals, because the meat was contaminated, so I gave them to my butcher to use as dog food.

'I also used to do rabbit pies here at the Green Dragon, but then people started going off them with all the fuss about myxomatosis.'

Among Pam's customers at the Green Dragon was 'an eccentric old boy' called Evelyn Light. 'He made a lot of money during the war, with wood – probably a lot on the black market – but was always dirty despite his wealth. He even bought a Rolls-Royce simply to put his calves in the back.

'One day John Biggs, the chief surveyor for Strong's, came in with his wife and family and sat at this lovely, long Cromwellian refectory table to enjoy some beautiful rump steak which I'd got in specially for a celebration. Then in came Evelyn and said to the Biggses: "Hallo, my ducks. You enjoyin' what you got?" Then Evelyn surged up to the bar and said to me: "I'll 'ave a pint of brown and a 'urry up." Well, to him a hurry up was a large Scotch which he hurried down before he went home.

'But while Evelyn was enjoying his drink he continued to watch the family eating. Then he went up to Judy Biggs and said: "You enjoyin' it, missus?" So she said yes and

*From the 1930s, a publicity poster painted by Robert Aichem*

just laughed, because she knew who he was. Then Evelyn went out and came back with his jacket on, put his hand in his pocket, brought out a handful of silage, shoved it under Judy's nose and said: "You enjoyin' that as much as my cows enjoyed this? 'Cos you're eatin' one of 'em!"

'Luckily the Biggses had a sense of humour and laughed like anything. I said: "Evelyn, take that ... stuff out of here." So out he went and took his coat off. Then he came back again, and said: "I'll 'ave some peanuts," but as soon as he started on those everybody covered their drinks up because Evelyn had only one tooth at the front and whenever he had nuts he'd talk at the same time, so the nuts flew everywhere.'

As well as the characters, there were many memorable incidents at the Green Dragon, both sad and humorous. 'One Boxing Day, when we had a big crowd in after the New Forest point-to-point, which is the oldest in the country, a family were sitting right here in this corner, an old couple and some younger people having something to eat. Suddenly the old boy went *aaahh* and passed out. I came round from behind the bar and helped lay him on the bench. Luckily, in the bar were two hospital sisters and they put a cushion under the man's head. Then one of them took me aside and whispered: "Phone for an ambulance and we'll pretend he's still alive." "But why?" I asked. So she said: "Because if we say he's dead they won't come but refer you to a doctor or under-taker." So that's what we did. Later we discovered that the man had recently been in hospital and the others had brought him out because they thought the change would do him good!

'On a happier note, I'll never forget the customer who had a glass eye and sometimes had to wash it, especially if the bar was very smoky. This particular day he went out into the gents' loo to see to it but was gone an unusually long time. Then John Cleal went out there and returned to say that this chap had dropped his eye in the basin and it had gone down the runnel and stuck in the end of a chute, but he couldn't get his hand in to recover it. Immediately I said, "Right, no one must go in there till we get the eye back, because they're terribly expensive."

'Then John devised a way to help. He got one of those little sticks like mechanics use to grind valves and asked around for a bit of chewing gum, which he pressed on the end. A couple of minutes later John reappeared with the eye stuck to the end of the stick, and the man it belonged to was overwhelmed. Immediately he dropped the eye in his beer, gave it a wash, popped it back in its socket, drank his beer and went. Of course, everybody in the bar thought this was hilarious, especially as all the men had to cross their legs while the eye was being retrieved!'

On leaving the Green Dragon, Pam took the Horse and Groom at nearby Wood Green, along with her younger daughter, Sarah, and her son-in-law. After a few diffi-cult years there Pam retired to a New Forest cottage, but remains closely involved with ponies and country life generally.

# FROM BUTCHER'S BOY TO ROCK STAR'S FRIEND

### Jim Rose of Worcestershire

When Jim Rose took over the Plough, a tiny pub in the hamlet of Shenstone, near Kidderminster, it was so run down that his wife sometimes cried with despair. Yet within a few years he transformed the former brewhouse for local peasantry into the regular haunt of the rich and famous: people from all walks of life were drawn as if by a magnet to the ebullient personality behind the bar. But no matter how high or mighty the customers were, all soon learnt not to overstep the mark, as the following incident – in Jim's words – clearly shows:

'This young chap's language was so bad I had to show him the door. I'd never allow foul talk in mixed company. I didn't mind a gang of men having a go over a game of crib, but when the pub was in full swing with ladies present I clamped right down.

'Anyway, two days later this chap came back and apologised, and thereafter we became great friends. Turned out he was John Bonham of the group Led Zeppelin, and at the time he was widely regarded as the world's number one drummer. He lived in the nearby village of Rushock and was some character, I can tell you, but a real wild one;

110

he used to do anything, would John. He was always taking home gallons of my bitter in old whisky bottles, and once he was stopped from getting on a plane with some.

'One day he invited the whole group over to my pub, and although I never liked their music, they all signed my guitar, which I still have.

'I have another treasured possession, too. I once beat John at snooker in his own house, and he said: "Damn me! I didn't think anyone would ever do that!" and gave me his cue.

'John was a real rock icon and fans used to hang around outside my pub till gone midnight, waiting for him to come out and hoping that he'd go with them to bless their house. In the end he died of the drink, at the age of thirty-one in 1980, after spending the last three days of his life in my pub. For years after I had no end of people come from America and other places to ask where his grave is.'

All this was a far cry from Jim's humble start in life. One of a council worker's three

*Jim Rose (right) with Bill Pratt, who preceded him as landlord of the Plough and lived until the age of 104*

children, he was born at nearby Chaddesley Corbett on 7 June 1925 and christened Edward James David. After leaving the village school at the age of fourteen he went to work in a carpet factory at Kidderminster, but 'the sun could hardly get in the window for dust' so he left after only two days and went to work for the butcher whose shop was next door to the Roses' cottage. So began a very tough time for Jim, as he recalls with some bitterness:

'My boss was the most miserablest, hardest man that ever lived. He'd come round and knock me up here at 5am, and in the summer I'd still be there at nine at night. I helped in the slaughterhouse and went out on the bike and in the van delivering all over the

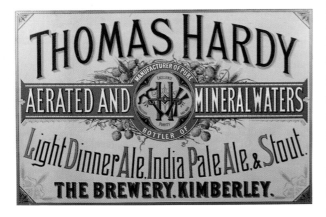

place, including to the local pubs. The lowest meat ration I can remember was 1s a head – 8d for fresh meat and 4d for corned beef. And at one time in the war no pub or restaurant was allowed to charge more than 5s for a meal. And for all my hard work all I got paid was 7s 6d for a *seven-day* week.'

After war service, Jim decided to work for himself, and although there were to be more tough times ahead, his great determination would see him through:

'I bought an old van and applied for a fish licence. I'd go over to Brum to buy big blocks of frozen cod, bring them back home and break them up to sell locally. Then, as my business grew, I got a bigger van and sold fruit and veg as well as fish. Marjorie helped me with this, even before we married in 1948 and moved to the end of the village.

'The Bathams had the Swan, opposite, and in 1954 Arthur Batham asked me to take the Plough at Shenstone. I said "God, that's small", and he said "A little pub full is better than a big one half empty". So I was persuaded to go, though for the first four years I still ran my van business while Marjorie looked after the pub.

'The place was in a very sorry state because the previous owner, Bill Pratt, was aged sixty-five and had lost all interest, especially since his wife had developed cancer. He had lived in the village all his life and was at the Plough for thirty-five years, having taken over from his mother-in-law as licensee for twelve years. In his day beer had been drawn in the corner of the room and was taken to customers, rather than them go up to a serving counter.

'At first hardly anybody at all came in and we took just 6s 8d on our first night and £42 1s 1d in our first week, compared with £753 on our last day and £4,009 in our last week, in October 1995. Mr Batham said "It's so bad I'll only ask for £1 a week rent".

'Our toilet was just a pit with a seat over for both men and women, and I found out later that even the men weren't using it – they all just went in nearby fields. So it wasn't surprising that we had days when nobody at all came in. Sometimes I'd return home and Marjorie would be in tears. She'd say "You left here for the fish market at 6am, it's now 8pm and I haven't seen a soul all day".'

The Roses were only the fourth family to live in that building since it became a pub in 1840. When they arrived, the inventory and valuation of fixtures and fittings included much of the old-beer making equipment; for example the 'fermenting house' still had a 250-gallon fermenting vat, two beer coolers and a tun pail, while the 'brewhouse' had a 200-gallon iron brewing furnace and a 150-gallon mash tun. However, the outgoing landlord had not brewed beer there for many years.

We cannot be sure exactly how Bill Pratt brewed his beer, but he probably made it somewhat more simply than along the following traditional lines. Crushed, sieved malt (roasted, partially germinated barley) is fed into the mash tun, already containing hot water, and stirred for up to two hours to produce a thick, sweet porridge in which the starches turn to sugar. As the resultant 'wort' is drained off from the bottom of the mash tun, the malt husks act as a filter. Any malt still left in the tun is then sprayed with hot water to extract any sugars remaining in the grain and to flush out the remaining wort. The 'spent' grain is often sold off as animal feed.

The wort is then run into a boiler, generally known as a copper or kettle, and boiled for up to ninety minutes or so with particular varieties of hop (to add the required aroma and flavour which give the beer much of its 'personality') to kill bacteria and separate the unwanted proteins which cloud the beer. Then the brew is run off through a 'hop back' which takes out the spent hops and waste proteins.

After cooling, the wort is run into a fermenting vessel and yeast added. Over a few days the yeast works vigorously on the sugars and the wort greatly increases in volume: then excess yeast is scooped off the top. Fermentation continues for a further few days, until the yeast is 'tired' and the brewer decides that the primary fermentation is complete. Then the beer is run into conditioning casks to soften the harsher flavours before being racked into casks and the addition of finings (a glutinous substance made from the swim bladder of the sturgeon fish) to take the yeast to the bottom and clear the liquid.

The Plough's inventory also shows just how slack the trade had become during Bill Pratt's time. For example, the entire glass stock consisted of only '2 large Guinness glasses, 2 plain mineral glasses, 35 stamped pint cups, 3 pint china cyder cups, 1 half-pint cyder cup, 13 half-pint glass cups – stamped, 2 half-pint thin ale glasses and 13 stout glasses'. The stock-in-trade was at an equally low level, the bar containing only '5 Spencer's minerals, 1 doz and 4 bottles half-pint Amber ales, 1 butler's case, 120 Player's cigarettes, 600 Woodbines, 4ozs Digger Flake, 7ozs Condor Pig Tail, 4ozs St Julien, 15 packets Rizla cigarette papers, 4 packets razor blades and 1 doz 3 Torch matches'. There was little more in the store, with '2 doz Spencer's minerals, 9 half-pint Worthingtons, 2 doz Spencer's lemonade, 1 doz large minerals, 2 doz and 8 pints Butler's Amber ales, 2 flagons Bulmer's cyder, 4 large minerals, 29 packets Nibbetts and 1 empty tin'. In fact,

Jim bought the entire stock and contents of the house for only £281 10s 9d!

The retiring landlord became a good friend of Jim's, even though he took the light bulbs which had been included in the inventory! Jim recalls:

'Bill Pratt moved just up the road and became a regular customer. When his wife died he was sixty-seven and then he went out and found his childhood sweetheart and married her. He lived to be 104 and he's the only person I've ever known to have had two silver weddings! He deserved a medal.

'The pub had been a double-fronted cottage and the Pratts lived in one side and served in the other, but when he went there we moved upstairs, thus doubling the bar space overnight. To begin with, we didn't sell any food at all, but later on Marjorie did hundreds of jars of pickled onions, and we were very famous for our pork pies made by a Black Country butcher.'

At first Jim only had a beer and cider licence and was refused a full licence – to include the sale of spirits – because he was not on the mains and the authorities said that his pump water was not pure enough to put on the bar for adding to whisky. This was despite the fact that when Jim had it tested by independent experts they found it 99.9% 'correct'. And there was further trouble when Jim's well ran dry. The brewery had to send barrels of water down to him for three months.

Throughout Jim's tenancy he was restricted to selling Batham's beer, as the brewery owned the place, but he was quite happy with this:

'In the old days us tenants suffered a bit because the brewers weren't really interested in the pubs themselves, only securing outlets for their beer. My old guv'nor was very reluctant to spend his money on improvements to the buildings. Batham's owned just eight pubs when I started, and even now they have only ten. Their beer has always been excellent, made to Grandma Batham's original, basic 1877 recipe and with a very heavy gravity. In 1954 it was only 1s 1d a pint for best bitter, and mild a couple of coppers less. When you'd had four or five pints of that you'd struggle to get the key in the hole. In the early days of the breathalyser seven or eight of my customers soon lost their licence.

'The strength of the beer didn't matter so much for some of my customers, as they came on horseback. It was always a very horsy area with big stables and good gallops nearby, and for years I kept meaning to put a hitching rail in. I always regret not having learnt to ride as I could easily have gone off early each morning. Instead I bought a vintage Triumph motorbike, which had been in the village since 1919 and was still in perfect working order. I rode this regularly for two years.

'However, I did once buy a racehorse, for 125 guineas in 1970. It was called The Roamer and was a bit rough at first, but Martin Tate – the trainer who sold it to me – soon had it in good condition. On its first day out it was second at Leicester, for which I won £60, and I also won £60 on the tote, so I paid for it with one outing. And second time out, at Stratford, it came first and I won enough to pay for my daughter's wedding, which took place on the following day. Then I sold the horse for a very good profit.

'Martin Tate used to lead his string of horses past the pub at about 6am, and every morning for thirty years he'd call out: "Come on landlord – don't lie in bed all day!" And when he retired his head lad carried on just the same. I should think everyone

*Holding court: Jim Rose often had his customers spellbound*

could hear him in this sleepy little hamlet, but most of the neighbours had a good laugh over it.'

At first Jim's opening hours were 10am to 2pm and 6 to 10pm, but then a new law allowed for an extra half-hour to 10.30pm in summer, primarily to benefit farm staff working late. However, this did not work out, as Jim explains:

'Not all areas had the extra half-hour, so at 10pm it was often like a race-track as customers rushed from pub to pub to get more drinking time. In the end it became so dangerous that the new regulations were abandoned.

'Because we were so tucked away, down a very narrow lane that led nowhere, we never had any passing trade and I could name every person going by. All strangers came by recommendation. People could spend an hour looking for us, yet I could stand in the car park and see high-sided vehicles going along the main road. But we were never snowed in because the local farmers always made sure that they could get to the Plough!'

As Jim's fame spread, the Plough was no longer only the haunt of farming folk, with two or three bikes propped up against the wall and the old police sergeant's helmet on

*Fond farewells at Jim's retirement party*

the counter as he supped his regular pint. The old faithfuls continued to come, of course, but so did people from most walks of life: as well as those well known in the racing world, such as Terry Biddlecombe and Peter Scudamore, Jim's customers included personalities from other sports, such as cricketers Ian Botham and Bob Willis.

Among aristocratic friends was Lord Newborough, with whom Jim shot on several occasions. When Jim visited Newborough's estate his lordship quipped: 'Now look, James – us landlords must stick together', which brought a wry smile to Jim's face as 'I was only the landlord of a tiny little pub and he was boss of 33,000 acres!'

Many of the regulars thoroughly enjoyed Jim's poetry readings. One enthusiast was millionaire John Scobie, who repeatedly asked Jim to recite A.E. Housman's *The Cherry Tree*, to which the landlord had introduced him. Indeed, such was the rapport between the two men that Jim was invited to address the congregation at Scobie's memorial service in Birmingham Cathedral.

However, not all callers at the Plough came for the fine beer or the entertainment. Several decided to help themselves to the landlord's property, although most were thwarted, as Jim recalls with great satisfaction:

'One time I outwitted thieves was when a customer tipped me off about two chaps fiddling my one-arm bandit, by trying to feed a strip of plastic through the coin slot. I crept up and caught them and wouldn't let them go until the law came, but I never did get reimbursed for the bag of money the police took away for evidence.

'Incidentally, I believe I was the first publican to have a bandit – previously only clubs had them. I also had a jukebox, though not for long, as it was taken out when we began to attract a better class of customer. Personally I don't mind a bit of background music as it can stimulate conversation if it's not too loud or objectionable.

'The only time thieves got the better of me was when I was talking outside and someone nipped over the counter and took the notes from the till.'

Over the years, Jim's success as a publican has been recognised on many occasions and in some notable guide books, such as the Automobile Association's *Britain's Best Pubs*, and in 1994 he was given a special plaque by the Campaign For Real Ale. At the presentation, CAMRA's chairman said: 'Mr Rose and the Plough have featured in twenty-three of our real ale guides during the twenty-five years we have been going. During the two years he missed out we came round and found his beer just as good as usual, but we thought we'd better give someone else a chance!'

With so many grateful customers, it was not surprising that Jim needed to 'borrow' the neighbouring farmer's field to accommodate all the cars at his retirement party. He was showered with presents from folk far and near, some of whom had been regulars throughout Jim's entire tenancy and had never patronised anywhere else.

Jim and Marjorie retired to the house in which Jim was born, at Chaddesley Corbett.

*Jim Rose – the landlord once renowned for reciting poetry as well as serving fine beer*

When I visited them there, it was so cosy, clean and comfortable that it was hard to believe what Jim told me:

'This cottage was just a hovel when my parents had it. Then it became a barber's shop and I used to come here for my haircut before it was left to become derelict. When we bought it we did it up and had tenants in for some eighteen years while we were still in the pub.'

How fitting that Jim Rose has returned to his native village and all its happy associations. Not surprisingly after such an active life, in which he claims to have 'pulled around two million pints – and drunk some of them, too!' he sometimes finds it difficult to sleep at night. He told me: 'I lie in bed and go through every house in the village and think of all the families who lived there. I can remember over 150 people here who have passed on in my time. Also, I have a bowling club photo taken at the Talbot, just along the road, in 1947; of the twenty-seven people in it only three are still alive, but I can name every one of them.'

Unlike Bill Pratt, after retirement Jim did not continue as a Plough regular, even though it is only two miles away; but he still has strong links with the pub trade. He can often be found behind the bar of the Huntsman Inn, at Kempsey in Worcestershire, when the owner, his elder daughter, needs a holiday. Now Jim has only one ambition left: 'To be shot by a jealous lover at the age of ninety-two'.

# GROWING UP WITH BOOZERS AND BODIES

*Freda Cheeseman of Kent*

When I spoke to charming Freda Cheeseman in her comfortable modern home, at Barming near Maidstone, it was hard to envisage the tough upbringing to which she had been subjected. She was born but a mile away, on 22 November 1915, in The Victory at East Farleigh, and by the time she left there, to go into service at the age of seventeen, she had seen more than enough of the seamier side of life. With her eighty-five-year-old husband William to prompt her memory, Freda recalled those testing times at the pub, so long ago.

'My father, Frederick Binskin, took over the pub from my grandfather, who bought it from Alf Enham. The story goes that it was a private house where Mr Enham made his own beer and kept a monkey that bit people. Apparently it took him years to get a licence, so when he won his battle he decided to call the pub The Victory.

'We had an outhouse where, over the years, quite a few bodies were stored because it was the only cool, secure place handy. These were people who had drowned in the nearby river [Medway] and very often nobody knew who they were, as there were a

*Freda aged five*

lot of tramps and very poor people wandering about in those days. But they were mostly suicides, and I expect that a lot of them came from the nearby mental hospital at Barming, which is the origin of the word "barmy" for people who are mad. I don't know how Father came to be custodian of the corpses.

'I started serving in the pub as a girl, and when I left school at the age of fourteen I carried on working there for a further three years. We had bare floorboards which we scrubbed every two days, and every night in the hop-picking season, when we were so busy. It was a miracle to me that the floor didn't collapse as it hardly had a chance to dry! And all around the front of the counter was a beaded-off area with sawdust for people to spit on. But this wasn't allowed in the public bar, which was just a partitioned-off area where fellows used to sit with their girlfriends. There were three particular boys who used to come in that bar and chat me up, and Dad encouraged this as it was good for trade. We didn't generally get many women in – just a few chaperoned ones for a glass of port.

'At that time I had a mongrel dog called Toby, who was a terrible thief, always going off and coming back with things belonging to our customers. One day I looked out and saw him running up the road with about 2lb of sausages strung out from his mouth.

'For many years we did a roaring trade, when loads of Londoners came down hop-picking on nearby farms. We were particularly busy at weekends, when lots of their friends and relatives came down to visit them, so we had a special room to serve them in. I already knew William from Farleigh school and long before we were married (in 1939) he used to come up to help. Often we were so busy we'd put two large barrels up on a stand, turn the taps on and run the ale non-stop into this big bath, so that we could fill the glasses, hand them out and take the money as quickly as possible, never stopping for hours on end!

'The village would be absolutely packed with pickers, from The Victory right up to the railway station. And they used to be so happy, singing all the latest songs like anything – you could hear them for miles. But they brought problems, too.

'Dad took their post in because they just lived in huts and had no proper address, so they'd come knocking on our door all hours of the day and night. The women used to fight a lot with hat pins, and once I saw this man tussle with Dad. I was only very young, and terrified when this chap was on the floor and tried to pull Dad down by the leg, but luckily he was rescued by someone else.

*Frederick, Freda's father, outside The Victory in the early 1900s. Walking up the road is Mr Smith, a keen gardener, on his way to collect the manure from the brewery's dray horses*

*Freda, happy in retirement*

'They were a rough, literally lousy lot, and didn't they smell! If they wanted to go to the loo they'd just drop their trousers and go anywhere! So we never allowed them to mix with our regulars, who had their own bit of garden. Mind you, some of the pickers could be nice, too. They'd come down year after year and when they saw me they'd say things like "Cor, ain't she grown". Most of them arrived by train and they were treated just like cattle.

'Another big problem was having glasses stolen or broken, so we only allowed tin pots in the pickers' room and Dad had these and all the glasses stamped with "F. Binskin, The Victory". But he still lost loads of them. And we had to walk all over the place picking them up because the pickers would just throw them down anywhere. In the end we had to say: "If you don't bring your pot back you won't get any more ale," but they'd just pick one up from anywhere, no matter who'd been drinking from it.

'We also did good trade with so many drivers and pickers coming down for all the fruit and vegetables grown in the area. And in those days there were lots of staff at the railway station, and they too came in for their pints. We also had a big room out the back where The Victory Angling Society held their regular meetings and what (for some reason) were known as smoking concerts. These anglers were always bringing coarse fish in from the Medway for our cat to eat raw.

'In Grandad's day the customers played skittles on the grass out the back, but in Father's time the main games played were shove-ha'penny and cards – mostly whist. Darts didn't come in till much later.

'Our beer came out by horse and dray from Style & Winch at Maidstone. One of our neighbours, Mr Smith, was a keen gardener and he'd always be around with his bucket to pick up the manure which the brewer's pair of Shires left in the road. As well as mild and bitter, they'd bring a small barrel of draught stout. We didn't sell any wine at all then and our only cider was bottled.

'Sadly, Mother was never a great help to Father, which is why I had to do so much. The only food she ever laid on was a bit of bread and cheese, if pressed. And although we had two spare beds, providing accommodation was not encouraged. One night there was one hell of a rumpus when this man staying crept into the other room with a woman in. Dad turned them both out immediately.

'When trade from the pickers and drivers faded off, and Mother got a taste for the "shorts", my parents went broke and had to leave, which was when I was twenty. But poor Dad already had cancer and only lived another two years, to the age of fifty seven.'

# THE FISHERMAN'S FRIEND
## Cyril Courtney of Devon

'They used to sell the little queen she-crabs from the boats down on the beach for 'alf a crown each. One day this visitor says to an ol' fisherman: "I'll 'ave a couple but I 'aven't got any change at the moment, but I'm goin' to the pub and I'll leave the money there for you," and off 'e went with the crabs. Later on the ol' fisherman comes in the pub and asks: "Did anyone leave any money for me, Cyril?" "No," I says. "Not five bob?" 'e asks again. "No, definitely not," I says. So 'e says: "Well – bugger me – if I'd a' known 'e weren't goin' t'pay I'd a' charged 'im ten bob!"

'These crabs were caught about three or four miles out and brought in to big store pots just offshore, near the pub. These pots had lids to keep the catch in, flitters [floats], and long ropes securing them to the beach, and when the men wanted more crabs for market, my pub or whatever, they would just team up and pull the pots in. Well, one day they's doin' this and this visitor who was watchin', not knowin' what the procedure was, said: "How on earth did they get in there?" So this ol' fisherman turns round an' says: "Well, miss, the last one in put the lid on!" Isn't that a wonderful story?'

These two yarns from Cyril Courtney reflect how closely he was involved with the local fisherman when he was the landlord of the Cricket Inn, in the tiny south Devon village

*Cyril's grandfather, Edward, took over the Cricket Inn in 1921*

of Beesands. Indeed, for many generations that rather isolated community was almost entirely dependent on crabbing. In his rich West Country accent, Cyril told me all about his family's long links with both crabbers and the pub, when I went to visit him and his wife Maggie at Kingsbridge, in the house to which they retired.

'Grandad was a gamekeeper before 'e bought the George Inn at Blackawton, near Dartmouth. When 'e sold the pub, in 1921, 'e bought the Cricket Inn, which 'e later sold to the Heavitree Brewery, who still own it but no longer brew beer. I was born at the pub, on 7 December 1930, but we soon moved to Cornwall when Dad, too, took a job as a gamekeeper and later 'ad a market garden there. But we often came back to visit Gran and Grandad during the 'olidays, and when Grandad retired in 1945 Dad took over as landlord. Maggie and I lived somewhere else in Beesands when I was in the building trade, but we often ran the pub while Mum and Dad went on 'oliday – I think the locals liked that – and I took over full-time as landlord when Dad retired in 1969.

'There's various ideas 'ow the pub got its name, but when you look at the village you'll see there's not much chance to play cricket there, and I shouldn't think there were even enough people to raise a regular team. We know there's been a pub 'ere at least since 1850, because it's listed in my White's directory for that year, and I think it was named after the old coastguard called Cricket. Perhaps it was a pair of the Cricket family's cottages which were knocked into one – there's certainly two staircases. But in the old days there was just one tiny bar.'

Cyril's very first memory of the pub concerns the spittoons. 'When I was six or seven I 'ad to empty 'em each day, and I was given a tiny little glass of sweet cider for doin' it. Course, cider used to be a very big thing here even in my time, and all the ol' boys used to 'ave their own pint cider mugs hangin' up. It was always more popular than the beer because of the price – probably about 8d or 10d a pint in the 1950s and sixties, when the mild beer was about a shillin' or one and somethin' a pint. And not long before that prices were much lower still: when Dad went there in 1945 a pound note would buy you forty-eight pints of cider, but when I left in 1995 you couldn't even get one pint for a pound.

*Cyril's parents, Archie and Rosie, during the time when his grandfather was still licensee*

'We always sold some sweet cider as well as a lot of the rough from local farms – many of the ol' fishermen were weaned on it. Oh yes, a real cider drinker was a cider drinker and no way was 'e ever goin' to drink beer. But we never really 'ad any big drinkers of any sort – mostly just the same fishermen comin' in every day at the same time for their two or three pints. Sunday lunchtime they'd come in at twelve reg'lar as clockwork, and we'd 'ave their drinks lined up waitin' for 'em as we knew exactly what they's goin' to 'ave. But come one o'clock – gone! – the lot of 'em: a ritual. See, they were fishermen, Brian, and for them eatin' was mostly any hour; but Sunday was different: that was when they 'ad to be 'ome prompt to sit down with the family. They very rarely put to sea on a Sunday. And I'll tell you summat else, Brian – in my grandfather's time no cards was allowed to be played in the pub on Sundays. Well, not that they weren't *allowed* to play, but they didn't *want* to themselves – nor darts.

'Incident'ly, one of the most popular games here is euchre. There's leagues an' all round yer and all the pubs have teams and tournaments. It's taken very seriously and is often very hard for an outsider to understand. But it's been goin' strong for as long as I can remember and it's very much a coastal thing: they say it came over with the ol' sailors from North America, which is where it started.'

(In fact euchre originated in Alsace, where it was known as *jucker* – probably the origin of the word joker, the extra card invented for the game of euchre and incorporated into British packs in the 1880s – and from there it was taken to North America. We do not know when it was introduced into the West Country but today it is the most popular pub and club card game west of Bristol and there is an English Euchre Association.)

'Anyway, one of these ol' cider drinkers was Dick Fay, who used to come down on the bus – when they ran to Beesands, that is – on the five o'clock from just a little way up the road; and he'd 'ave 'is few pints in time for the return bus at about quarter to ten. Well, one day just as the bus came 'e said: "Can't stop – got to go for a piddle." So when he'd gone out I emptied his glass into another and filled 'is own up with a mixture of ginger wine and water, made up to the same colour and level of the cider as 'e left it. In come Dick. "Hurry up – bus is waitin'," I says. "I know the bloody bus is waitin'," he replies. So 'e downs 'is drink in one and off 'e goes out the door and round the corner. All of a sudden the door opens again and 'e says: "Bugger you." But when 'e came back the followin' day 'e was laughin' all over 'is face.

'Dick used to go and pick winkles and sell them to people, often in my pub, in a pint pewter mug which he'd dip in a bag and say "Here you are – tenpence, please," or whatever. Anyway, one day when 'e left 'is bag of winkles in my porch I emptied it out and filled it up with shingle. Course, when 'e comes out 'e dips 'is mug in without lookin' and 'e says: "Good God, what's goin' on 'ere? You bugger Cyril, I know 'twas you."

'Do you know, Brian, there's a lot of these ol' men I wished I'd got *all* their stories. The ol' fishermen that I 'ad in my pub I could sit and listen to them for ever – it's such a shame they're gone now. They were magic with their yarns – 'twas like havin' a book read to you. They specially used to love talking to visitors, and these strangers would ask them questions which I 'adn't even thought about. They were all crab fishermen, all

126

*Fishermen, at Newlyn in Cornwall, discussing the day's catch*

men of the sea, but they all 'ad somethin' different about them and all 'ad their lovely names – Johno Steer, Wackey (Lewis Crocker, a lovely feller) and old Buster – William Lynn – all wonderful characters. And if you ever wanted 'elp they were there to back you up – real men. I loved 'em because they were part of our life and so good to us.

'There's one or two of the ol' crabbers 'bout still, but it's mostly much larger boats come out of Dartmouth and Salcombe now. In the old days it used to be just two men to an 18ft boat, and they'd own that boat between them and fish with about fifty or sixty pots nearly every day. Now these big boats 'ave three men on board and pull about six or seven hundred pots, but they're all mechanical assisted. Oh yes, it's all big business now and lots of crabs go to Spain and France. But in my little village of Beesands for as far back as I can remember the men would always land the crabs on the beach, pack them in boxes and barrels, put 'em on the special lorry for Kingsbridge station and send them up to Billingsgate by rail. It's the finest crabs in Great Britain there, in Start Bay. Smaller numbers of boats have gone out from other places, but Beesands was always known as *the* crabbin' village. There was forty men and twenty boats went out of Beesands, so we always 'ad plenty of thirsty customers.

'Now I stand to be corrected on this, but the biggest crab I can remember at the pub was about 12lb, and we've 'andled 7–8lb crabs quite recently. They were always sold by weight, but I can remember some as cheap as sixpence. The men would get their money back from Billingsgate by registered letter into Beesands Post Office. But that's gone now, along with the village shop. Now the nearest shop's about 3½ miles away, as there's nothin' to support one with so many 'ouses empty for much of the year and almost everyone ownin' a car. Now it's nearly all 'oliday cottages. You see that row of 'ouses in that painting there, which was done by one of our customers for us? Well, I think there's about thirty-two all told, but now twenty of them stand empty in winter. You see that block of four there? Well, just one person lives in them for 'alf the year. But not so long ago, in each one of those little two-bedroom cottages there used to be a family of eight or nine, and they all relied on the crabbin'.

'We always sold crab sandwiches in the pub, for as far back as I can remember, and could get fresh crabs almost any time we wanted as they were on our doorstep. We killed 'em, cooked 'em, dressed 'em, the lot, and there was no need to store 'em in a tank. The only difficulty getting 'em was during a long period of rough weather, but people understood that – there was no storing 'em frozen.'

When I asked Cyril if the fishermen ever got fed up with eating their own catch, he replied: 'Brian – those fishermen *loved* crab: I've never known one who didn't. Maggie's brother-in-law was a fisherman and 'e'd even eat crab when 'e got up at three o'clock in the mornin'! Those men went to work very early, you see, with the tides. Sometimes they caught a little bit of wet fish – they'd shoot long lines and bring in ray or turbot, stuff like that. But crabbin' was their industry. They even used the dead crabs – the ones which came in dead or dyin' – for their garden manure. From the pub you'd 'ear the ol' wheelbarrow goin' along with its steel wheel and you'd say: "Hallo, there's old Arthur takin' 'is load of spider crabs along to bury 'em down." Oh yes, 'twas a life on its own there.

'The local people also used to 'ave licences to catch salmon in the sea. The men would sit beside their boats, waitin' with their seine nets, while another sat up top o' the hill, lookin' down into the sea. Tom Gillard was the best of all as he had wonderful eyesight an' 'e would spot any fish goin' on by, sometimes just by the different colour if he couldn't see it clearly in the water – oh yes! Then when 'e spotted something 'e would whistle for the men to launch the boats, and when they were in position 'e would put 'is 'and out for them to shoot the net. Mullet was caught in the same way, too.

'When Grandfather was at the pub, back in the twenties, they used to catch the salmon just the same, and the licence ran from sunrise on Monday to sundown on Friday, so Saturdays and Sundays you weren't allowed to catch 'em – you 'ad to give the fish two days free. But if a salmon ran up by on a Saturday you could be damn sure they weren't goin' to ignore it. However, in those days there was a bailiff to watch out for – Salmon Jack we used to call 'im, and 'e'd come up the shore on 'is motorbike. But as 'e came up through Torcross the butcher there would give my grandfather a shout on the telephone to say 'e was on the way, and then Grandfather would warn the fishermen by hanging a yellow duster out the pub window. When the men saw this some of them would hold the bailiff up by distracting him, while the others would either bury the salmon on the beach or come away from it altogether.

'But in the old days we didn't serve any cooked salmon in the pub. We always ate well ourselves, with plenty of things like Gran's great big hams hangin' up and huge local cheeses. Also, we always 'ad the Torcross butcher call on a Tuesday and Friday. And I'll tell you somethin', Brian – his father called on my father and his grandfather called on my grandfather, all the way back to 1921. But in those days there wasn't so much demand from tourists. Course, transport weren't so easy then and goin' from A to B took a long time – you wouldn't 'a come down 'ere this mornin' in the time you made it, Brian. It's not so long since it always took eight hours from 'ere to London – 240 miles at 30mph. So it was well into the late 1960s before there was any real demand for pub meals down this way, which started with scampi or chicken an' chips in a basket. The ol' fishermen were fascinated by this and some couldn't get over it. In pubs like ours they'd only ever known sandwiches and a few pasties, apart from crisps – tins and tins of packets in bloomin' great stacks. But they was real crisps then, with salt in little blue bags which were just twists of paper.

'And don't forget, when I took over from Father there was no such thing as lager in that pub, an' no Bacardi or fancy drinks like that. Our men were brought up on real ale. In 1969 we had just the one keg bitter – from Gibbs Mew of Salisbury – and even that wasn't very popular. It was all Heavitree mild and bitter – real ale – and I 'ad to tap every cask, wheel in 18s and 22s [gallons] and throw 'em up on stills. But then the keg beers came on strong everywhere, pushing the real ales out, and gently, gently, those ol' boys who were beer rather than cider drinkers were weaned onto them. Now, even though the real ales are back in favour again, these ol' boys don't want 'em – no way. I guarantee that if you went in that pub today the majority of men there would drink keg Worthington. Oh yes, very few of the locals would drink real ale.

'That reminds me of a story. This chap comes into our pub an' says: "Can I 'ave a pint please – a little drop of beer topped up with water." So I says: "Well, I've never been asked for that before. Do you always drink it?" And he replies "If you 'ad what I've got that's all you'd drink." "What's that?" I ask. "Fourpence," 'e says. Now you can believe that if you like.'

Ever a great practical joker, Cyril once got into the local papers with one of his pranks, which he recounted to me with great glee. 'When it was our silver wedding we were goin' to 'ave a do on the Saturday night, but on the lunchtime we also got all the staff in to 'ave a drink with us. Among them was Edie Rendle – the little ol' lady who lived next door and worked for us, cleanin' and helpin' in the kitchen – and her husband Jack. Well, as they was all sittin' around chattin' Edie 'appened to say 'bout some pigeons she was cookin', so I thought ... interestin'! Course, in those times the fishermen often used to shoot the woodpigeons on the days when it was rough and they couldn't put to sea.

'Anyway, I made sure Edie and Jack were all right, with plenty to eat and drink, and I thought, now's the chance. I went out the side door, knowin' full well that Edie would never have locked up, crept into her kitchen, took the pigeons out of the oven and brought 'em back round to mine, carefully shutting everything behind me.

'After a while Edie says: "Jack – you better go an' see 'bout the pigeons." "All right, Mother," 'e says and off 'e went; but 'e soon came back saying: "What pigeons, Edie? There ain't no pigeons in our oven." "Bloody ol' fool," she says, "of course there's pigeons in our oven – I put 'em in there myself. Go back again, you silly ol' man." So off 'e went, but when 'e came back a second time 'e was lookin' a bit fired up: "I'm tellin' you, Edie, there ain't no pigeons in our oven." "Course there are, you damned ol' fool – I'll 'ave to go and see to them myself." But it wasn't long before she was back, laughin' 'er 'ead off and sayin': "You're right, Jack, there ain't no pigeons in our oven." Course, by then she was more than a bit merry as we'd been puttin' brandy in 'er snowball [Advocaat and lemonade], so she says: "Oh bugger the pigeons, it's that bloody Cyril done that – 'e bin in and got 'em." By then the 'ole bar was in uproar.'

However, life at the Cricket Inn was not always an endless round of merriment for the Courtneys. On the contrary, the pub suffered some very sad and serious incidents during the family's long tenure.

'One Sunday afternoon in 1942 a German plane came in low and dropped a bomb on its belly on the open space which was known as the village green, so the bomb bounced and exploded right next to the pub. It killed seven and injured twenty, including my aunt who was sitting in the pub window having a cup of tea when the 'ole lot came straight at 'er, so she was blinded. But the strange thing is you never hear anyone mention it now. It's as if it's been wiped from the village memory, even though there's a plaque about it in the church. Course, the pub was very badly damaged.

'One night in 1979 we 'ad lots of torrential rain. Now look at that picture, Brian – you see where the hill's comin' down and that sunshine's catchin' that area there? That's where it all ran through. I woke in the night to all this clankin' and crashin' and thought, what the devil's goin' on? Bang, clonk, bang, clonk, and lots of breakin' of glass. So I went down and heard all this noise in the yard. Well, when I opened this door – still 'alf asleep, mind – into the little passageway, there was all this water, about 4in deep. The rain had come straight off the hill into our backyard and through the bar – it was in the back door and out the front. It was like a river and there was no way I could stop it, so I called the fire brigade out from Kingsbridge and they pumped and pumped for hours on end. Everythin' was red with the soil washed down and the mess was terrible, but I suppose we were quite lucky in the pub. The fire brigade were so marvellous – they even took all our carpet up to dry – we managed to open at eleven the next morning. But thank God there was no cellar: we had a stone floor and all our beer was stored in a little place above ground. The awful noise I'd heard was caused by the earth bank slipping and crushing an asbestos hut up against the brick wall next door, breakin' all its windows.

'That was an awful night, also with the high winds and the sea ripping up stones and smashing bedroom windows. Some people were out their cottages for four months with all the damage. Today it's all very different there as they built a proper sea-wall in 1992. Some people

*Cyril Courtney with two of the old cider mugs*

don't like it, though. It might be safer and tidier but a lot of folk used to like sitting on the old piles of loose rocks 'avin' a pint or just watchin' the world shuffle by.'

When I left Cyril I drove out along the narrow coastal roads to visit the pub which he had told me about with such passion. The weather was exceptionally murky and miserable for August, so damp and disconsolate holidaymakers sought refuge in the bar, with honest, old-fashioned home cooking rather than picnics on the beach. Old photos on the pub walls bore testimony to the long relationship with fishermen, and – thankfully – the very plain decor had not been tarted up. However, through the window you could no longer enjoy a view of the sea because of that imprisoning new sea-wall. And while my pint was satisfactory it was a long time coming, and there was no great welcome from the overworked staff or the few people who appeared to be locals among the grim-faced, rained-off trippers. Indeed, when one man came in just after me his chum jokingly called out to him in deep Devonian: 'Are you a member? You'm can't come in if you'm not a member.'

I suppose this was a fairly typical scenario in one of so many pubs which have suddenly been swamped by droves of 'outsiders'. But how different it seemed from the positively friendly way in which Cyril used to treat everyone. He told me: 'I always used to make sure that a stranger never stood alone. I would always go over to 'im and get 'im to ask me questions, and then I'd gently put another question to, say, ol' Frank Crocker – 'e was always there – to bring someone else into what we were saying. Then I'd slowly move away and the next thing you'd know they'd be engrossed in conversation, and that stranger would love it. I never wanted anyone to feel out of place or be lonely – that's a terrible thing in a pub. I'd always go and say hallo to everyone.'

With such a caring attitude Cyril Courtney was not only a true fisherman's friend but a kingpin of the community.

# NO TIME FOR NIMBYS
## *Ruby Griffin of Buckinghamshire*

In countless rural backwaters, the plain old local catering for mostly humble farming folk has been transformed by the arrival of relatively sophisticated 'incomers' with the cash to commute. While the great majority of them are thoroughly nice chaps who want no more than a good pint of real ale and a home-made pie, or simply 'to belong', some can be difficult. Instead of remaining diplomatically quiet until they have gained local acceptance, they burst through the bar door with big guns blazing and wanting to change everything. And woe betide any cock that crows and spoils their sleep for if it does it is likely to be blasted from its perch by double-barrelled bureaucracy. These few unfortunate individuals can be surprisingly intolerant and ignorant of country ways and practise what veteran landlady Ruby Griffin calls nimbyism – adherence to the principle of 'not in my back yard'. Over a fine pint of her Fuller's London Pride, Ruby told me all about this phenomenon as well as many of her other experiences as a landlady for fifty years in the Buckinghamshire village of Steeple Claydon.

'There was one ol' chap 'ere 'ad what we call a "phantam", a cross between a pheasant and a bantam, and that caused no end of complaints from the nimbys. Even the poor ol' cows are frightened to moo any more. Course, it doesn't 'elp that people don't seem to stay long in the village nowadays. Just as they're comin' round to takin' to us

(above) *The Fountain and general stores (left) early this century*

132

they're movin' out again, to take up some new job in another part of the country. And with all the infillin' with new houses that's brought 'em 'ere there's no room to keep the animals like we used to.

'Also, a lot of my ol' regulars had to move out through a lot of unemployment, and then these richer people could snap their houses up at bargain prices. Many of our customers who weren't farmers used to work at the Calvert brickworks, which opened in 1900 and once employed over 1,100 workers, and when it closed in 1991 threw 'eaps of people on the dole. More jobs went when the abattoir closed down. Some went to the pie factory at Aylesbury, but then that closed, too, and this became what they call a distressed area. And a lot of people left 'ere could 'ardly afford a pint, so it's been tough for pubs, too. All those brickworkers used to be very good customers because they drank such a lot when they got so hot. They'd either walk over or cycle up of an evenin', and it was the unmarried ones that was the big drinkers as they 'ad more money to spare.

'The Black 'Orse was done away with years ago. Taurus Close was built in its paddock. Then the Prince of Wales closed, but now that's open again. The Crown closed and then re-opened, but now it's making way for more houses. The Sportsman closed about four years ago, while the Phoenix and the Seven Stars both changed 'ands loads an' loads of times. I'm the only one whose sort o' stuck it out all these years. There's a very old rhyme about the pubs in Steeple Claydon:

> The Black Horse kicked the Crown,
> then drunk the Fountain dry.
> The Sportsman shot the Prince of Wales
> and made the Phoenix fly.

We don't know who wrote it but I've known it for as long as I can remember.'

Unemployment is no stranger to the area. For hundreds of years up to the early eighteenth century, the population of the village (which owes its existence to the clay used in brick-making) remained constant at about 200–400. Then, with better living conditions generally, came a sudden increase. The 1801 census revealed a population of 646 living in only 104 houses, and by 1831 this had risen to 881, many of whom could not find work. At that time there were just two pubs, the Sportsman and the Milk Pail, as well as a 'beer-shop'. But there had been others long before that. A surviving manorial roll of court findings for 1558 records that one Alice Synll, 'a common tippler' (alehouse keeper), was overcharging for beer and thus 'in mercy' (liable to a fine). Most of these early publicans would have had to supplement their earnings through farming or other occupations.

Ruby was born on 2 May 1927 at Sandhill, Middle Claydon, and her father worked at the Calvert brickworks. After school she worked at the local Co-op until she was twenty. In 1947 she married Cyril Griffin, the son of the landlord of the Seven Stars, a river-ford inn at Twyford, on the outskirts of Steeple Claydon.

'The Seven Stars had been in my husband's family since the 1880s. It was kept by my father-in-law's father-in-law, who came here when they were buildin' the railroads, as did my grandfather. Cyril and I gradually took over as father-in-law became increasingly ill.

'Our beer came from the old Aylesbury Brewery and we sold a lot of bottled light ale, brown ale and Guinness as well as mild and bitter. I always remember servin' up my very first Guinness – it was a hot day and I just couldn't get it in the glass properly, which was unfortunate as it was a Sunday and that was the day when we were very busy with lots of people 'avin' the time to walk out to us from surroundin' villages.

'We did a bit of food then, especially sandwiches – and toast an' eggs, as we 'ad plenty of people like builders callin' in the mornin' till about half ten. We always 'ad loads of eggs as we kept about a hundred battery hens and lots of other birds and animals, includin' about thirty geese, seventeen ducks, three cows, six sheep and loads of pigs, all on land we rented.

'When my 'usband was a boy, undertakers often used to stay at the Stars, and there was a shed at the back where they'd put the hearse and coffin overnight. Well, one day young Cyril got very interested in 'avin' a look so when all was quiet 'e got in the 'earse and lifted the coffin lid. Unfortunately 'e 'ad more of a shock than 'e bargained for because not only 'ad 'e not seen anybody dead before but also just as 'e lifted the lid his grandfather shouted at 'im!

'There was one room at the Stars where the drovers used to stay when they were takin' sheep to Buckingham. Its windows were very low so they had iron bars across to make sure that nobody left without payin'.

'They were tough people there in the old days. My husband's grandfather actually used to carry the small (9-gallon) barrels of beer in a sack from Calvert station out to the Seven Stars. At the time he also worked on the railway and could take a shortcut along the track.

'There always used to be a lot of rivalry about what people could do in the old days. My grandmother's father, Harry Carter, had a dispute over a wager with a man down at the Crown. He 'ad to carry a 2¼cwt sack of beans that they'd 'arvested all the way to Calvert bridge and back to the pub without puttin' it down once. Well 'e did this but this man claimed 'e was a yard short where 'e put the sack down, so Harry did it all over again, about 'alf a mile each way. You try doin' that! I've tried just liftin' a 2¼ cwt sack of wheat off the ground and that was 'eavy enough, an' beans would be 'eavier than that as they're really solid. Mind you, they was quite stodgy fellows in the ol' days, what I'm like now!

'In the ol' days we used to 'ave weeks of rain, but we don't 'ardly 'ave a shower now. At the Stars we 'ad a mill and a backwater of the Ouse behind us, so we had a lot of flooding, but the ol' builders were really crafty and the bar flagstones were specially laid on gravel, so that the water could drain away quickly. But there were no sewers then so we only ever 'ad clear water to worry about. We always knew when it was goin' to flood because we 'ad a marker in the yard, and when it reached a certain level we knew it would be in that night. Then as soon as the pub was shut we'd put the wooden chairs up out the way on the tables, which were just rough trestles then, and the best comfy chairs were taken upstairs.

'When the people after us 'ad tiles put down in the kitchen the water couldn't get out easily when it flooded up the drains. And when they 'ad sewers put in they could be

*Ruby with her late husband, Cyril*

in real trouble if it flooded. They couldn't just go upstairs for a while, like we did, but 'ad to move out a few times.'

Ruby and Cyril left the Seven Stars when her father-in-law died, and in 1955 they took the Fountain, in the centre of Steeple Claydon. At the same time they acquired the shop next to the pub, which had been an ambition of Ruby's since she worked at the Co-op. The shop is now closed and Cyril died in 1980, but Ruby remains at the Fountain, working alongside her married son Clive, who took over as licensee in 1997.

'It was originally a thatched cottage, public house and bakery, with butcher to the right and stables to the rear, where Oliver Cromwell took shelter on his march north. An old customer told me that the pub, which went back about 400 years, used to be called the Star, but people kept gettin' confused with the Seven Stars, so when it was burnt down and rebuilt in 1905 they decided to call it the Fountain. They chose this name because a spring within the pub's grounds used to provide the villagers with clean water. You can still see the remains of the disused well.

'The ol' landlady we took over from 'ad been at the Fountain for twenty-five years, but then she remarried and lived to be 100! I'd known 'er from my young days when I delivered groceries to 'er from the Co-op and she always used to give me a little liqueur glass full of claret.

'When we came in everythin' was terrible, really, with dark paint all over and cherry wallpaper upstairs. We took the ol' spittoons out, and the wooden ridge for the sawdust on the floor round the bar – I wasn't 'avin' that! But I kept the black lead range in the kitchen, where I thought the floor tiles were black but it turned out they was just filthy, and after a lot of scrubbin' with Vim and Ajax I discovered they was really red. And there was this table in there that was so big my young children could walk under it pushin' a small pram with a doll and cat in. We broke that up to make a kennel for our first of three Alsatians, which we got after someone took a week's takings from a drawer in the bureau. And another time someone just walked in the back door and took some savings stamps books and the tin with the thrift club money off the table.

'We brought some of our animals with us as there was still lots of space, with many allotments, and most of these 'ouses round 'ere weren't built. So we came with two sows, our hens, a dozen cockerels and 'alf a dozen ducks, and more or less kept ourselves in food; but we bought some meat, of course, as you don't want pork all the time any more than you want chicken every day.

'Our rent was very low, but it still went up fourteen times from what the old lady was payin', so she must 'ave been payin' peanuts. Fortunately we were busy from the word go, but to get every drop of beer you served you 'ad to run down five steps into the ol' cellar. But 'twas all in mugs with 'andles and I could carry four pints at a time. And I got on with everyone well because I already knew them well, having always lived nearby. And at Christmas we used to do a lot of beer and wine deliveries, before the off-licences got goin' and people started fetchin' booze in from France.

'The Fountain was then owned by the Aylesbury Brewing Company, who had acquired it from the Brackley Brewery. Now it belongs to Fuller's, whose London brewery, by coincidence, is called the Griffin.

'We've 'ad some great characters here, includin' ol' Jack Butler, who was in the theatre as a tap dancer and a caller. He often danced in the pub an' got all the others goin' with the piano when we 'ad sing-songs on Saturday nights. Then there was Miss Hoff, the signalwoman at Claydon station. If you went to an away darts match you couldn't come back over the crossin' after 10 at night because she wouldn't open the gate. She'd take anyone on if they'd 'ad a few drinks an' gave 'er a bit o' lip. Everyone was terrified of 'er.

'My Cyril often used to get called out to different things where so many people knew 'im and 'e was easy to contact, bein' in the centre of the village and 'avin' a phone when there weren't so many about. Sometimes 'e 'ad to go to 'ouses when someone 'ad died, and carry 'em upstairs or fetch the doctor. The thing is, we were often the first people incomers got to know and they 'ad nobody else to ask for help.

'One thing I specially remember that upset me was when this woman came tearing down 'ere one lunchtime and said, "My dad's in the pond!" So my 'usband and 'is friend

*The village pub often hosted a good old sing-song on a Saturday night*

got a rope an' this ol' door from our garage and walked over to the pond, which was used to water the allotments, and you couldn't get a vehicle down the narrow path leadin' to it. Turned out this poor ol' boy, who was a lovely chap, 'ad committed suicide because 'e thought 'e was in the way livin' with 'is family. But when they brought 'im back down past me to put 'im in our garage until the police arrived, you should 'ave seen 'im flat out on this door, all covered in green algae from the pond! It put me right off me dinner.

'We've 'ad some tough times, too. In 1976 we 'ad a fire in our grocery shop, through an electrical fault, and the insurance didn't cover much of what we lost as we were very over-stocked for Christmas. Twenty years of work went in one afternoon. We carried on for another ten years, but then became a victim of the supermarket era and closed down.

'Then, in October 1987, I was in the pub bathroom when I 'eard this almighty bang and thought the boiler 'ad blown up. But when I came down and looked in the kitchen I couldn't see much at all with all the dust and smoke, so I called Clive at 'is bungalow an' said: "You'd better come down, the boiler's blew up." So down 'e comes to investigate, and then 'e says: "It's not the boiler, it's the chimney come down on the kitchen table in the hurricane and there's a ton of stuff up there waitin' to fall at any moment! Don't you go back in there again."

'Unfortunately, like so many others in the old days, the brewery we 'ad then didn't really care about its tenants. People were often left for ages with leakin' roofs or whatever, so I was without my kitchen for six months, before it was put right. During that time all I could do for hungry customers was a roll and cheese, and I 'ad to go up to Clive's for me own dinner every night.'

Despite all these hardships and changes in society, the Fountain remains at the heart of the community, providing a valuable meeting place for young and old. With lots of customer participation in sports and games and frequent live music and other events, it is still a 'local' in the truest sense, a family pub where troubles and successes are shared by all. With Clive now successfully setting the pub's course into the twenty-first century, Ruby remains at the helm, as a bulwark against nimbyism. Understandably, she is 'slowin' up a bit with poor circulation in the legs after all the standin' behind the bar for over half a century', but she still has the warmest of welcomes for locals and newcomers alike.

# A HAVEN FOR ALL

## The Eight Bells of Belchamp Walter, Essex

Wife-swappers, nymphomaniacs, sex-mad men, drunks, the poor and the sick were only some of the many extroverts and unfortunates who once found a sympathetic ear at the Eight Bells, in the Essex village of Belchamp Walter. But then, in Joan Gore the pub did have a particularly understanding landlady, who did so much for so many people over the ten years till the doors were closed to the public for the last time, in 1977. Surprisingly, Joan was forced to leave through ill-health, for now she is one of the most vivacious and youthful OAPs I have ever encountered. Aided by her daughter Susy, who also used to serve in the pub, Joan told me all about her life and eccentric customers as we sat by the fire in the old Pembrokeshire farmhouse where she has lived for the last fifteen years.

'I was born at Wivenhoe and after various jobs, including the Land Army, I married in 1949. My husband John became the actual licensee of the pub when we took over in 1967, but he didn't have much to do with it as he continued with his full-time job as a civil servant.

'We didn't know how long the place had been a pub but the building probably dated back to Queen Anne, and there were hooks in the wall at the front, where horses used

139

*Vivacious octogenarian Joan Gore and her daughter Susy*

to be tethered. We had the odd customer come by horseback even in our time, as we were right out in the wilds there. We learnt quite a lot about the pub's history from some of our older customers.

'There was this dear old boy called George Chatters who bought a farm with the proceeds from running the pub during the war. Apparently, through some fiddle he always had lots of beer when rationing was on, so the pub was always full. They say he was so busy he often ran out of mugs so people would bring their own jam jars to drink from.

'Some time after the war they stopped making beer at the pub and the owner, Mr Ward, bought a brewery at Foxearth, about five miles away. The Eight Bells beer had been made in a very small room which had been sealed off, and we found it when we took the wallpaper off while decorating. There was still a pile of roasted barley in there and buried in the barley was a very old-fashioned gentleman's blue suit, which you could poke your finger through. Everything was covered with rat droppings and it was very spooky.

'Also in the old days a man used to come round with a horse and cart selling kippers once or twice a week. He would go in the pub and all the old boys in the snug would buy the kippers and cook them over the open bar fire. Apparently they used to stink the place out.

'Another thing we learned from old George in the pub was that once a year, into the early part of this century, all the men and boys from the village would walk down towards Sudbury and meet up halfway with the men and boys from Ballingdon Hill to fight each other until they were exhausted. He didn't know why this started, but it could have had something to do with the fact that the villages were in different counties, Ballingdon Hill being in Suffolk. Also, even when we were there the local people, including our customers, were very intermarried and protective of their own patch.

'When we arrived at the pub it needed quite a lot of attention. For a start, our cellar was always getting flooded and we had to put boots on to get the beer, so we often kept customers waiting. Eventually we complained to Mr Ward and he had a slatted floor put in. Also, the brown lino on the floor of the public bar was very dried out and cracked, so we took it up and put carpet down. Unfortunately, our regulars – we only had five at first! – didn't like it so three of them stayed away for weeks. Only Buster and his girl-friend Celia stayed because they had nowhere else to go to do their courting. And they didn't drink that much either. He just had half of bitter while she had a Lucozade.

'One very poor and very dirty old boy used to drink the dregs out of people's glasses, which the landlord before us used to tip into a tray under the beer pump and save for him. Old Albert also used to have all the cigarette stubs out of the ash trays and he'd take them home, break them up and roll his own from them. We didn't continue with either practice, but used to slip Albert the odd pint on the quiet.

'When they had shoots from Belchamp Hall, the ground where the pub car park is now used to be lined out with hundreds of hares, but in our time there were very few hares left. Later on we catered for pheasant and partridge shoots, the beaters having their bread and cheese in one bar while the Guns had something like steak-and-kidney pie in another.

'The local gamekeeper – Olly Barrel – was a wonderful character, only about five feet high. Whenever he was unwell he always ate a slice of bread which he'd poured boiling water over and put a lot of pepper on. Also, he always wore a celluloid collar because years ago he'd broken his neck when he fell off a haystack, yet he ran everywhere when he was past seventy. When he came in the pub he'd say: "Put a tiger in my tank, Joanie," by which he meant put a glass of ginger wine in his light ale. And when he'd had a lot to drink he'd jump up and down on the spot, then say: "That's jumped it down," meaning his neck!

'Sometimes Olly used to come up and get me to make the soft leather things which they used to put on the reared pheasants' wings so that they couldn't fly. He always said that his fingers were too clumsy for the job, so he sat and watched me do it while he drank his beer along with Major Tuffel, who ran the shoot.

'Olly had a tiny wife – Edie, who couldn't have been more than 4ft 6in. She often used to come in the bar and ask for chips. When I cooked them and brought them out to her, she'd take them all out of the basket, break them in half and lay them in rows along the bar.

'One day Edie got so drunk at another pub that when she got home she fell backwards all the way down the stairs. After that she became very thin and everybody thought that was the end of her. So every morning I used to mix her up an egg with sugar and sherry and a glass of milk, and take it down to her cottage, to try to get her going again. Fortunately she did recover, but it became embarrassing because when she'd had a drink she used to call out to the whole bar: "My landlady's saved my life – she's been down every day with sherry, egg and milk for me." But she was a dear old thing, always making and drinking this ghastly rhubarb wine, which was ever so potent.

'Across the road a little bit further down was a dear little cottage, and living there were Maisie and George Phillips, a tiny man who had ten sons, but they weren't by Maisie. At first they lived in London and George had plenty of money because he was a dentist on Harley Street. After George said goodbye to his wife and set off for work each morning he'd pick up Maisie, who'd be waiting for him round the corner. She'd get in the car and cover herself up on the back seat with a blanket, and when they'd got out of the area she'd uncover herself and climb in the front with George. Unfortunately for George, one day they did this and Maisie said: "Well, we've got shot of the old so-and-so now," but Mrs Phillips was hiding in the boot! Then the Phillipses got divorced.

*Throughout the country the pub outing was always a popular event*

'George and Maisie then led a very high life, eating at all the smart restaurants, but they drank so heavily they got through all their money and had to give up their London house. They moved down to the cottage near us and George took a part-time job in a dental practice in Sudbury, which was our nearest town. And every day, as soon as George had gone to work Maisie would come into the pub and quaff the beers. In fact she was always first in, both morning and night. But with all the drinking, they neglected themselves and their very old cottage. One day when they were in bed together the whole front wall of the cottage fell out – top and bottom! But they were all right.

'One day Maisie was in the bar when George was very ill, and she had to use our phone to contact the doctor. I asked her if she'd given George his medicine as she'd been told to. She said : "Oh no, that's not for another hour." Then Susy and I had to go shopping, into Sudbury, so I told Maisie that she could stop in the pub to use the phone. Also, I knew she'd be better off there because she wouldn't have a fire alight at home.

'When we came back, about an hour and a half later, Maisie was still there and she was as drunk as a newt because she'd been helping herself to the optics. She said to me: "Oh, Joanie, you've come to see George – how sweet. Come along upstairs and I'll show you." So I told her: "Maisie, you're not in *your* house but at the Bells!" "Oh, am I?" she

142

said. And when I asked her if she'd phoned the doctor or given George his medicine, she replied: "Oh no, I'll do it later." But poor old George died the next day!

'Maisie never had a fire and hardly ever had any food in the house. After George died we watched her get thinner and thinner, so any time we had a bit of a do in the pub we'd save anything left over – sandwiches or whatever – for her.

'Poor old Maisie. She became so frail and thin and was always so drunk that when the wind blew she had to hold on to the hedge to get home. It was disgraceful that she lived in that way while her daughter was on the council in the next village. In the end I was so cross I phoned this woman and said: "How can you call yourself a caring council worker when you leave your mother to starve and freeze?" Fortunately she listened to me and came over to take Maisie back with her.

'Another thing that shocked us was the wife-swapping among our customers. There was one farmer, who we'd better call Fred to save any embarrassment, and another we'll call John. Now John's wife was a cripple and he used to carry on with our barmaid. But John was also very fond of Fred's wife so he often used to visit her when Fred was away, and whenever he went to bed with her he would leave Fred a bottle of whisky on the sideboard. When they made their arrangements Fred would go with a young lady we'll call Mavis, who was a teacher. What really surprised me was the completely open way they discussed all this in the bar on the very first Sunday we were there, saying things like, "Who are you going to have tonight, then, John?" We watched them pair off and go, and we were dumbfounded because we weren't even used to pubs, let alone that behaviour.

'Susy once had a fanatical admirer and when she chucked him he was very upset. One night he even sat outside her bedroom with a shotgun! Eventually, to get even with her he burgled us while we were out. We knew it was him because both Maisie and Olly saw him go. The police searched his house but it was never pinned on him. Then he joined the Army, but when he came back to see us at the pub two years later he was a changed man. The Army had turned him into a nice, smart chap, but he brought his girlfriend with him and not only was she called Sue but also she looked like Susy.

'Another odd person was a man we called Sexy. He had a sweet factory in America and came over to promote his goodies. His aged aunt was the honourable somebody or other in Gestingthorpe, and she was supposed to book him into the poshest hotel in the area, the Swan in Sudbury; but by mistake she booked him in with us. When he came I think he was trying to sow all his wild oats in about three days: he was truly shocking.

'The first night this American joined some others dancing to the jukebox in the public bar. He was mauling the girls about, and, of course, our barmaid was there having a lovely time because she liked that sort of thing. Then he asked me to show him where his room was, and when I took him up he politely asked for a glass of water; but when I returned with it he grabbed me by the arm, whisked me into the bedroom and tried to kiss me. So I shoved him away and said: "You've got the wrong one here – you'd better go back down and see if you can find somebody else." After that, when we were cleaning up in the bar while he was having breakfast, or at any other time, I always made sure that my Susy and I were never with him by ourselves.

'Another visitor who surprised us was the man who booked in for six weeks' bed and breakfast and insisted that when he came he did not want "anything to do with the family"; yet he ended up staying for seven years and marrying Buster's girlfriend, Celia!

'We had another strange visitor apparently from the States. One day this well-spoken Yankee turned up and asked if we could put him up for a night or two, so I said yes, and he ended up staying for three weeks. Then two policemen came into the bar and asked if we had a man who said he was a Red Indian, I said yes and they said they were sorry, but they'd have to take him away as he'd been on the run from some institution and had been staying at different places without paying for his keep. "But you can't do that," I said, "he's quiet and well-behaved and he's paid on the dot at the end of every week. And I'm sure he's an Indian because he looks like one and he told us he's the chief of the Iowa tribe. He even showed us his headdress and other regalia. "Oh no he's not," they said, and with that they went upstairs to get this dear little chap and then they marched him away.

'After a while we changed the snug into a music room for young people. We put a record player in there and the local boys decorated it themselves, with a black ceiling

*The country pub has always been the focus for a wide range of social events: here the members of an anglers' society quench their thirst after a day's fishing*

and lots of posters. It was really nice for them and most of them were well-behaved. Then just before closing one night these three notorious brothers came in and took their drinks into the music room. After about fifteen minutes we heard a lot of crashing and banging in there but Susy and I were alone and we wouldn't go in there because we knew of these boys' terrible reputation with girls and drinking. We had to wait for them to go, and when we went in we were horrified to see that they'd broken every glass and all the records and had trodden them into the floor.

'I phoned the local policeman and told him that it must have been these brothers as they were the only people in the room that night. Also I said that one must have a badly cut hand because there was blood over everything. But he did nothing at all about it because he was as frightened of them as everybody else was.

'This policeman came from the next village and he never interfered with us much. He'd always come round about a quarter of an hour before closing time and say: "Everything all right in here?" We'd say, "Yes thanks," and he'd say, "OK – I shan't trouble you again tonight." This was just as well because our customers always wanted to stay to about one o'clock most nights and to three on Sunday. But in the end we knew them so well we'd say: "Right – you can serve yourselves, but here's a pen and pad. Please write your name down and record all the drinks you have and you can pay us on Monday." Then we'd go to bed and we'd hear them clanking about with bottles and things below. It was rather nice to think that we could trust them like that.

'We had two football teams and the players were more like my sons. When they got tiddly we had great beer mat fights, flicking them at each other, but we had to stop that when someone got cut. The boys often had to stay well after hours because I made them have lots of cups of coffee and something to eat while they sat round the floor in my living room until they were sober enough to go.

'Another lively crowd were the local Irish community of three families. When they came in the pub they'd sing along with Jim Reeves on the jukebox, and then they'd start crying before going back to their homes to play all the old patriotic songs.

'Later on we started to have live music, which became so popular with people from nearby towns the road outside would be blocked with cars. Also, we established a supper room with a late drinks licence to twelve, and this was very successful with people coming from up to thirty miles away, apart from the time I set the kitchen on fire while cooking chips and nearly choked the parrot to death.

'Then the breathalyser came in and mucked up that supper trade. But soon after, we had to leave the pub anyway as I became ill through doing too much and Susy left to get married. Ward sold out to Bass Charrington, but sadly the place never reopened as a pub. One couple tried to turn it into a glorified restaurant but they went bust while the alterations were going on.

'On reflection, it sounds as though all our customers were either drunks or very immoral, but I must say that the majority were very nice people and I do miss pub life.'

# THE LOONY LANDLORD

*Roger Killeen of Somerset*

Whereas many village inns were established to accommodate the masons building the parish church, the Phelips Arms is thought to have been provided for masons building a place fit for a very high-flyer. After building the magnificent Montacute House in the late sixteenth century, Edward Phelips went on to become Speaker of the House of Commons under James I and led the prosecution at the trial of Guy Fawkes. Coincidentally, the inn still has strong political ties, but the current landlord is more concerned with teasing than treason. Indeed, there is considerable justification in calling Roger Killeen loony as he is a leading light in the Monster Raving Loony Party, having founded the Yeovil and District branch and acting as its chairman since 1993.

With Roger's imaginative and extrovert support, the local MRLP candidate, John Archer ('chosen because he looked the part and he was the only one with a top hat'), polled 309 votes at the last General Election – not bad going since the local MP was Paddy Ashdown, leader of the Lib Dems.

I asked Roger if Paddy was one of his regulars. 'No fear,' he replied. 'He won't come too close with our Loony link, but he has been known to pop in for the odd Mars bar while out on a walk.' Perhaps he was partly put off by Roger's letter to him, suggesting an alliance between their two parties.

(above) *Roger Killeen (back centre) with MRLP founder Screaming Lord Sutch (front centre) and other loonies*

## 10 DOWNING STREET
LONDON SW1A 2AA

24th March 1994

Dear Mr Killeen,

Thank you for your letter to the Prime Minister of 1st March suggesting an alliance between the Monster Raving Loony Party and the Conservative Party. I have been asked to reply on his behalf.

This is not a proposal the Prime Minister would accept and I am sure that yet again the Conservative Party will do better than opinion polls predict.

Yours sincerely,

Lucy Miller

MISS LUCY MILLER
Political Office

R Killeen Esq

---

## HOUSE OF COMMONS
LONDON SW1A 0AA

The Office of the
Leader of The Opposition

8 September 1994

Dear R.T. Killeen,

Thank you for your letter of congratulation to Mr Blair.

I am afraid however that we cannot accept your offer of an alliance between our two parties. You may have better luck if you try the Conservative Party, though given their performance in government it looks as though you are already exerting plenty of influence over them.

Yours sincerely,

Pat McFadden

Pat McFadden
Assistant to the Rt. Hon. Tony Blair MP

R.T. Killeen
The Phelps Arms
Montacute
Somerset
TA15 6XB

---

## YEOVIL & DISTRICT MONSTER RAVING LOONY PARTY

The Phelips Arms
Montacute
Somerset TA15 6XB
Tel: 0935 822557

17 March 1995

Mr Neil Kinnock
The European Commission
Brussels
Belgium

Dear Mr Kinnock,

We of the Yeovil and District M.R.L.P. (membership 303) wish to express our admiration for the European ideal and the single European currency.

However, we feel that the word "Ecu" is an ugly word for a noble concept, and therefore submit the following proposals for the consideration of the European Commission.

Please consider the following:
1) 10 Wellingtons to the Waterloo
2) 10 Napoleons to the Nelson
3) 10 De Gaulles to the Churchill

It is our considered opinion that these proposed names for the currency of the future reflect both the balance and history of Europe over the last two hundred years, and will stand us in good stead over the next two hundred.

Your views would be appreciated.

Yours,

R. KILLEEN
Chairperson

---

## EUROPEAN COMMISSION

Member of Cabinet
Office of NEIL KINNOCK

Brussels, 1st April 1995

R. Killeen
Chairperson
Yeovil & District
Monster Raving Loony Party
The Phelips Arms
Montacute
Somerset TA15 6XB
United Kingdom

Dear R. Killeen

Neil Kinnock asked me to thank you for your letter of 17 March. He appreciates your support for the European ideal. He would like to build on your suggestion in the following manner: -

10 Lord Byrons to the Dylan Thomas

10 Will Carlings to the Gareth Edwards

10 Felicity Lotts to the Geraint Evans

10 Elton Johns to the Tom Jones.

Yours sincerely,

Chris Boyd

# THE PUB

The staff at your local will try to ensure that your visit is pleasant and enjoyable. However, if you wish to be greeted with a warm welcome on your second visit, the following advice may be of use:

1) When the front door is locked and the sign hanging from it says closed, please do not ring the door bell to ask if we are open.

2) Questions like:

'Is the garden outside?'

'Do you have a toilet?'

'What's that in the ham sandwich?' may cause annoyance.

3) Female customers whose first language is English are allowed to talk to the bar staff direct, the use of a male interpreter being totally unnecessary.

4) If your first question is 'Can I be difficult?' the answer will be no.

5) When using the toilet, please do not pick your nose and then wipe your finger on the wall.

6) If you are clutching a large piece of laminated card which lists a variety of meals with prices alongside them, the question 'Is this the menu?' will probably elicit a sarcastic response such as 'No, it's a Rochdale telephone directory'.

7) When you have just walked through the front door, please do not enquire what the weather is like in the garden.

8) You may think your children are cherubs, but we think they belong to the junior Baader Meinhof and are using our premises as an assault course in preparation for an attempt at global domination. Please keep them under control.

9) Husbands and wives do not hold hands or grope each other in public. People having a bit on the side do. It is obvious, embarrassing and silly. Please control your hormones.

10) This may come as a surprise to some people, but your fellow diners do not wish to hear about your colostomy.

11) The waitress will incur less serious burns to her hands if you can remember what you ordered.

12) When your meal is delivered to you, the waitress would be extremely grateful if you removed from your place-mat your hands, drink, keys, road map, guide book, cigarettes, mobile phone, Filofax, handbag and the drip mat which you have been studiously mutilating for the last five minutes.

13) When asked how you would like your steak cooked, to reply 'In a frying pan' is no longer regarded as either novel or funny.

14) The same applies to those people who wave empty glassses around and enquire: 'Can you get a half in there?'

15) Our catering department have devised a new concept called 'The Menu'. Everything they do is on 'The Menu' and everything they don't do is left off 'The Menu'. You may find it useful to consult 'The Menu' before ordering.

Not surprisingly, John Major flatly rejected a similar proposal in 1994, as did Tony Blair when he became Leader of the Opposition in the same year. Their replies, reproduced here reflect the enthusiasm and invention which Roger has brought to his calling.

The letters form just part of an intriguing collection which polite customers may peruse if they call for a pint. And I must emphasise the word 'polite' because, after twenty-three years in pubs Roger does not suffer fools gladly, as his witty guide for visitors makes clear:

Not surprisingly for an active 'politician', Roger has sometimes 'put his foot in it' during his nine years at the Phelips Arms. He described some of his gaffes as I quaffed a few pints of his exceptionally good Palmers 200 premium ale and Palmers best bitter (IPA):

'One day I asked this woman when her baby was due, only to discover that she wasn't pregnant! Then there was this blind man who told me he'd been a customer for twenty years and I said: "You must have seen a few changes!" Equally embarrassing was the time when I took an order into the kitchen and the wife asked if I would take a couple of sweets out while I was there. "Sure," I said, "what are they and where are the people sat?" She said: "It's a gooseberry fool and a treacle tart for the two ladies in the window." But after I went over to them and said: "Who's the fool and who's the tart?" I wanted the ground to swallow me up.'

On another occasion it was a Phelips Arms customer who made a great gaffe. 'A well-known politician and his wife arrived and paused at the door. The wife, who kept track of local affairs while he monitored matters of national import, quickly scanned the assembled throng. She pointed a few people out to him, saying: "He's the dodgy planning permission, that one's complaining about the housing list, and that's Don – wife's been unwell." So the politician strode up to Don, shook his hand in a statesmanlike way and said: "Hallo, Don. How's the wife?" Don replied: "Oh, she's still dead, still dead." '

There have been many occasions when Roger has brought his impish sense of humour to bear on other unsuspecting customers.

'A toff came into the bar one day and took an age looking at the hand-pull pumps. Eventually, he said: "What's the nearest thing you've got to a real ale?" So I looked carefully at the pumps, decided that the one dispensing the Guinness was the nearest to the real ale and sold him a pint of it. He left happy enough.

'Then there was this fellow from a visiting skittles team who came up to the bar and asked for a pint of Toby. I told him that we didn't sell it. "But I only drink Toby," he muttered. "We *don't* have any," I said again, and he replied: "But that's all I drink." So I said: "How many Fs are there in Toby?" He said: "There ain't any F in Toby!" So I said: "Isn't that what I've been trying to tell you?" '

With Roger at the helm, it's no wonder that MRLP meetings at his pub are well attended. The branch has some sixty members, including astronomer Patrick Moore. Also, to boost funds, cards have been sold to tourists as curious mementoes of their visit to Loony land, so now members range from a Thai in Bangkok to a Mormon in Salt Lake City.

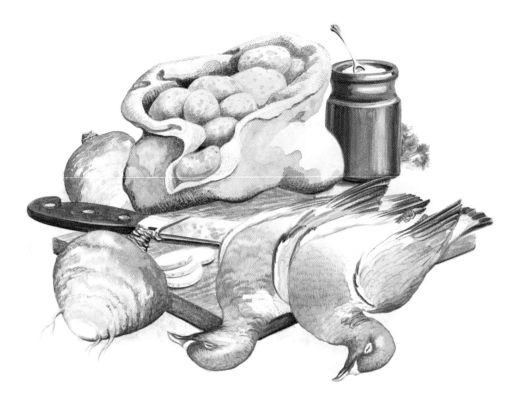

# CONTRIBUTING TO THE COMMUNITY

*Mary Leak of Lincolnshire*

In a generally high-profile position, the country publican often has the opportunity to become a kingpin of the small community. But few have served their villages better than Miss Mary Leak, so it was fitting that, in 1978, she received a Brewers' Society 'Local Life Award – for licensees who have contributed to a richer and fuller life for members of the community'. When she was landlady of the Black Horse, Donington on Bain, during the fifteen years to 1984, she started holding events to raise a great deal of money for charities such as cancer research. Her pub quiz nights and stuffed-chine suppers attracted as many as 300 people and raised as much as £1,600 in a single year. But that has been only one aspect of Mary's good-heartedness in the three Lincolnshire pubs where she has worked, all in the Louth area.

The daughter of a farm worker, Mary was born at Appleby, near Scunthorpe, on 23 December 1918. She was only eight when her mother died and then she wanted to become a nurse, but like so many other working-class girls of the day she ended up living in as a housemaid, at North Willingham.

From 1935 to 1939, Mary worked at the Royal Oak, Cawthorpe, where she lived in after a while and did bar work as well as housework. At first, the pub relied mostly on farmers and labourers for trade, but after the outbreak of war it became much busier, with an influx of RAF men from Manby. As Mary recalls: 'It was a time when we lived for today, with lots of sing-songs round the grand piano.' Such get-togethers were most important in bolstering the spirit of the local community at a time of great stress.

While the Royal Oak was still 'very old-fashioned' in the 1930s, it was not the most primitive pub which Mary visited. That was the Clickem Inn at Swinhope, 'where you had to part the cobwebs to get in, and it was always so dim with paraffin lighting and lots of smoke from the fire that you couldn't see if you had the right change'.

*The Royal Oak at Cawthorpe, where Mary worked in the 1930s*

After working as a Land Girl and in forestry during and just after the war, Mary went to work and later lived for thirteen years at the Waggon and Horses, in South Reston. There she was able to continue her close relationship with the countryside and animals, as well as hunting.

'The pub was owned by Hewitt's Brewery and their managing director, Mr Donald Birt, was a joint-master of the Southwold, so they met at the pub quite regularly, as they did later on at the Black Horse. At both pubs I always gave 'em a stirrup cup of port and brandy – "tally-ho lotion" I called it. You treated 'em to that, but in return they looked after me ever so well.

'Hunting day was always busy and I never shut from opening early at about ten in the morning right through to bedtime, although you weren't supposed to. And when the field returned after hunting I always had two or three gallons of my home-made soup ready for 'em, before the serious drinking started.

'At South Reston I sometimes reared fox cubs in an outbuilding. I called one pair Port and Brandy. They were very young ones which had been dug out – their numbers had to be kept down to help people protect their poultry – and if they were for someone else you didn't keep them long or else they wouldn't be faithful to the permanent owner. But I did keep a few on, including Charlie who lived for seventeen and a half years and another who lived for twelve and a half years. I also tamed an otter which I found on the beach at Saltfleet. She was called Tarka and was with me for years, but died after I gave her a myxy rabbit which I picked up from the road. But we always had plenty of food there as we also had a smallholding and sold ducks.

'As I helped run the Waggon and Horses I started to drink more, and the harder you worked the more you drunk. My drink then was rum and blackcurrant and one night George Moses said to me: "I'm glad you're not my girlfriend – I wouldn't want to take you out." "Why's that?" I asked. So 'e says: "Well, I bin watchin' you tonight and you've drunk 'alf a bottle of rum." But I've only ever been drunk once in me life: I woke up

*Mary has had terriers all her life, and has always named them Diddles. When she was young and naughty she would crawl into the kennels 'because the dogs would always protect me and nobody would come near'*

next mornin' with the skin off the palms of me 'ands where I'd crawled 'ome from a wedding at the Waggon, before I moved in there.

'When people used to drink a lot more, gout was more common. I always knew when one chap had it. He used to come in the Waggon and say: "No, I don't want me usual bitter Mary – just pass me a flagon of cider and a glass." That was always the quickest thing to cure gout.'

At South Reston, Mary's skill as a cook came to the fore, although she remembers that in those days most pub food was fairly basic.

'I never bothered much about exotic food – 'twas all sandwiches at first. In any case I didn't have time for much else then, with all the cleanin' and bar work to do. But I did make a lot of pigeon pies, which were very popular, and some meals were very much a community effort, with the keepers shooting the birds, one man contributing a bag of potatoes and another bringing, say, a bag of swedes to go with them. When I made a batch of pies I just took the pigeon breasts and legs, added a nice lot of fat bacon and beef and stewed the lot together until it dropped to pieces. Then I filled enamel dishes and covered them with a nice thick pastry crust.

'One day this old gypsy lady came round to the pub selling pegs and things and then she suddenly died. Almost the next day, her relatives burnt her entire van and all the beautiful things inside, which was their tradition.

'Another old gypsy lady lived permanently in a caravan near the pub. It was absolutely filthy and every so often the council sent someone – she would only talk to one man – to tow her onto clean land. If any of my customers went too near her gate she'd throw the contents of her 'goes-under' [chamberpot] over them. She was a very strange woman and always came round the Waggon asking me for one of my tame foxes. That embroidery of a fox on my wall is one she did for me.'

Although she was a very generous landlady, Mary would never stand any unruly behaviour. 'There was this ol' boy – Billy Marsden from Sheffield – who had a lot of cattle waggons and visited all the markets. He used to come in the Waggon and Horses and get terribly drunk and rude, till one night I opened the door and told him to go and never come back. So off 'e went, but a minute later he pushed the door open and said: "One day you'll need my money," but I never did. Some of these people think that because they've a bob or two in their pockets they own you and you'll do anything they want. But you must never give in to 'em.'

In helping to make a happy pub central to village activities, Mary held many a late session and is proud of the fact that she sometimes 'let the customers out as the dawn was coming up'. However, she 'always looked after the police, makin' a friend of 'em all with cups of coffee whenever they called', and in so doing struck a happy balance between law and disorder.

'One Good Friday evening the sergeant came in just after eleven o'clock and said: "What on earth do you think you're doing still open?" So I said: "I've been waiting for you to arrive so that I could ask if we can stay open like the shops are allowed to now." So he said: "Come on, you know you can't – see 'em all off home. Now I'm goin' to the

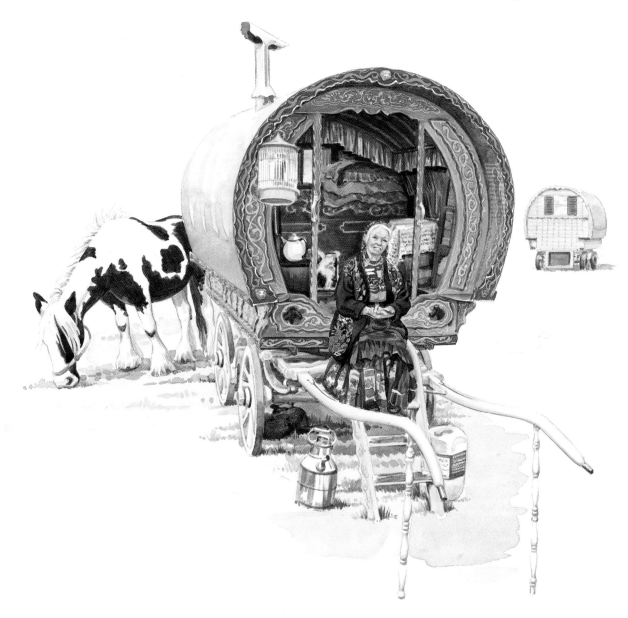

telephone box and when I come back in five minutes I expect to see the place empty." As soon as he'd gone, I filled all the customers' glasses up and they trooped into my private sitting room.

'When the sergeant came back he said: "You got rid of that lot quick." I said "Aye. Now what do you want to drink?" He said: "A pint of mild, thank you," but I persuaded him to have a whisky as well. However, I told him that he'd have to go into the sitting room to drink it. "If the others can't stay in the bar then you can't either!" So through he went, but when he opened the door and saw these twenty or so other drinkers squashed in there, his face was a picture.

'We used to get snowed in quite a bit, but one year at the Black Horse it lasted for weeks on end and the farmers were even fetchin' me beer on tractors. One morning the police inspector from Louth rang me and said: "Now, Mary, how are you getting on?" I replied: "Not so bad, thank you," and he said: "I'm ringing you because I thought you'd know better than anyone if anybody needed anything. You know it's almost impossible for us to get out." "I know," I said, "I get up each morning and peel me tatties and do me bakin' early so that I'm all ready for when the men come in from their snow diggin' for a warm-up of rum, baked potatoes and hot bread rolls." He says "You what?" So I says: "Oh yes, they must 'ave their tot of rum when snow diggin', and when they gets cold again they can come back for another as well as whatever they want to eat." So the inspector says: "You are a cheeky bugger, Mary, tellin' me all this – you know darn well I can't come out there and catch you." I says: "I do." But it was all local people out there diggin' because the council men couldn't get anywhere near us, and someone had to keep 'em goin'. When they eventually dug us out, on a Sunday, we called it "the relief of Mafeking".'

When Mary retired from the Black Horse, the brewery bought her a nearby cottage at Donington on Bain, but nine years later Hewitt Brothers sold up, so Mary was forced to move into a council bungalow. Throughout her retirement, despite some ill-health, Mary has remained closely involved with the welfare of the village people, not least in caring for the sick and as secretary-organiser of groups such as the Evergreens and the Forget-Me-Nots, whom she always gave the warmth of the bar.

*Good fun at a darts match at the local*

# HALE AND HEARTY

One cold and frosty morning in the sleepy hamlet of King's Walden, Hertfordshire, locals were astonished at the sight of a slumbering body, partially covered by a sleeping bag, projecting from the back of an old camper van in the pub car park. They soon realised that nothing was amiss …it was only old Artie Hale, who hadn't quite made it home after a heavy session at the Plough! He'd play safe after an evening in the pub and stay close by, waking next morning to cook his breakfast of beef or conger eel steak, or a locally poached fish, on his little stove.

Now aged seventy-four, Artie can be described as a 'serious ' patron of the Plough – he's been drinking there for as long as anyone can remember, and now lives in a house just down the lane. A lifelong bachelor, who retired as a toolmaker at the age of sixty-five, he is now almost as wide as he is high, and fondly recalls his more 'mobile' days:

'The local lawman was a real friend, and when I camped at the pub he'd bang on the van window to make sure that I got up in time for work. Even the police superintendent sometimes acted as my alarm clock! I was caught drink-driving once, though, and banned for a year. My local bobby told everyone "Fancy them doing old Artie!", and he almost apologised on behalf of the police!'

Artie first visited the Plough – 'along with every other pub in the area' – in 1938, when he was an apprentice. The following year he volunteered to become a paratrooper, his subsequent postings including India, Burma and Pakistan. He remained a regular after the war and saw eighteen months' service in Korea.

The current landlord of the Plough – appropriately named John Game – continues to cater for a very sporting community. Artie chuckles as he remembers his years in front of the bar:

'A few years ago John raised some baby owls, and one, called Chiquita (it ate a chick a day!) would sit in me 'at while I played dominoes. And that's not always the quiet game it's made out to be – one day ol' Ted Dobson, the farrier, made the wrong move so this chap 'it 'im and it ended up in a right old fisticuffs. In the end they had to be separated – and they were both over seventy! Then this other chap barred himself from the pub until Ted had died.

'Another of Ted's wrong moves was when he turned left instead of right when he took a horse into the pub, and got it well stuck – it took 'im ages to back it out!

'We've always been close to nature here, with a lot of huntin', shootin' and fishin' nearby, so the pub's customers would include anyone from Denny Goodge, always with a ferret in his pocket, to Lord Chichester and his friends. I suppose that in the old days there was a fair amount of class distinction – I'll never forget that when landlord Jack Day's father retired from the local estate after fifty-seven years' service he was given just one pound note! But today most people mix well and we enjoy the occasional chuckle – like the time this stranger was going on about how to catch pheasants with raisins, not knowing that he was advisin' the headkeeper!'

*(above) Artie Hale with his own painting of the Plough, which he presented to the landlord, and the engraved tankard presented to him by brewers Greene King for his great loyalty to the pub*

# LILY LIVES ON...

*At the Barley Mow, Kirk Ireton, Derbyshire*

After landlady Lily Ford (née Simpson) died in 1976, her powerful presence appeared to live on at Kirk Ireton's Barley Mow, where she spent her entire eighty-nine years. When her successor introduced a modern till it inexplicably failed to function, as did a borrowed replacement, so a simple cash drawer was reverted to. Apparently Lily despised anything modern, and it was as if her ghost was ensuring that nothing would change. Even today some customers still sense her presence.

As it is, Lily would be delighted with the way things have turned out, for landlady Mary Short has proved to be an equally excellent custodian. Indeed, since 1976 she has been so successful at preserving and also enhancing the Barley Mow's timeless character that the pub has been given CAMRA's star rating as one with 'a rare and unspoilt interior of historic interest'. This is all the more remarkable because virtually none of Lily Ford's furniture or other possessions remained in the building after her death. Mary explained:

'We lived nearby and bought the building at auction, but what we took on was just a shell as the entire contents were sold separately. Just about the only things left were

Lily's poker and her shortbread biscuit tin in which she kept her money. In her later years, when she had bad arthritis, she sat by the fire and acted as cashier, right up to a week before her death. You paid her; and then her assistant, Luke Wood, would serve your drinks through the hatch. But if she knew you well enough she'd let you get your own beer. She ignored VAT and wouldn't have anything to do with decimal coinage, so most people gave her a note and she kept a stock of florins and shillings to give them change. How she juggled it around I don't know, but I'm sure she didn't lose out.

'Lily played the church organ and on Sundays provided tea and biscuits in the pub for the ladies who didn't drink, but she was very authoritarian, often unjustly accused people of under-age drinking and would never allow anyone at all to stand in the bar. However, there's no doubt that Mrs Ford's example has helped me to keep a firm hand here, so I've never had any trouble.'

*A late Victorian painting of landlady Lily Ford as a young girl*

The Barley Mow is a tall, handsome, predominantly Jacobean stone building with a sundial dated 1683 high on the front wall, though the back is even older. It was probably once the manor house and so far its use as an inn has been traced back to 1826. It is a true haven of yesteryear with its shuttered, mullioned windows, low-beamed ceilings, tiled and wooden floors, antique settles built into the panelling, wonderfully quiet and peaceful atmosphere, and a simple wooden counter behind which lie tempting casks of real ale, including the excellent Hartington bitter, brewed by Whim Ales at Buxton. No music or games machine intrudes to spoil the gentle art of conversation or a simple game of cards or dominoes.

When Samuel Dean bought the tenancy of the 'publick house' in 1854 he paid Isaac Slater a total of just £76 19s 0d for all the stock, furniture and equipment. In those days he was buying malt and hops to brew his own beer and he paid 10s 6d a gallon for both ordinary and strong gin, 11s for a gallon of peppermint (presumably for flavouring drinks), 15s for a gallon of Jamaican rum and 16s for a gallon of Islay whisky. He would not allow smoking in the pub and all pipes had to be left outside.

Lily Ford's father, William Simpson, took over in about 1874. In the following year he hired Sarah Ford at nearby Wirksworth for £13 (subsequently her annual wages were £7 7s per annum) and fitted her out with a cap at 3s 6d, an apron at 1s, buttons for 5d, a dress and buttons for 9s 6d and lace and velvet at 2s. But these amounts were deducted from her pay, as were the sums of 7s 6d for a doctor's bill, 6d for brandy for her mother, £1 1s for dressmaking and 4d for elastic for her boots.

When Mary Short and her architect husband took over, there was only one bar, so they turned Lily's downstairs bedroom into a bar parlour and also opened up a third room. While the work was in progress the pub was closed for seven months, during which time (and later) Mary acquired antique furniture in keeping with the building. Sadly, after a while some of the more valuable items had to be removed because of the rough way in which they were being handled. Even so, you still get the feeling that nothing has changed there for centuries.

In 1976 the pub sign was missing, presumably having fallen down or blown down in Mrs Ford's day, so Mary had a replacement made, basing it on photographs showing the

old one. This was particularly important at the time because of competition from another pub in the village, the now-closed Bull's Head. But nowadays the sign is almost obscured by the large tree in front of the building, so you would hardly know that there is a pub there at all.

Today the Barley Mow has more of a mixed clientele, Kirk Ireton having grown from a small agricultural community with five farms centred on the village in 1976 into a much larger place housing many professional commuters and having only one farm.

Some links with old ways remain, such as the gypsy woman who still calls to sell brushes and other items, but now she comes in a van and even has a mobile phone!

Most of the old characters have long gone, but from time to time amusing things are said or still happen down at the Barley Mow.

'This old boy in the bar had been to an auction and tucked away quite a few drinks, and after a while he offered to sell some of his land to another customer. They agreed a price and spat and shook hands on the deal in the traditional way, and the young farmer asked me to lend him the £100 deposit, which I duly handed over. But news travels fast in a small community and when a young relative of the old man heard about the arrangement he came rushing up to the pub in quite a state, terribly worried that much of his inheritance was disappearing fast. He tried to get Frank to go home but the old man refused to go, staying all evening and occasionally breaking into song. Eventually the distraught relative was very relieved to discover that the prospective buyer had only been teasing!

'Then there was the customer with a tin leg, who lived in an old van in the local disused sandpits, even right through the winter. I think he was escaping from a wife somewhere and he was quite well read, but one old farmer remarked: "The trouble with him is he doesn't really know anything – he's only read it in a book!"

'But perhaps my favourite customer comment was from a lady who said: "The nice thing about having a video recorder is that it takes the pressure off watching television."' No doubt Lily Ford would not have approved of either device.

*The Cheshire Cheese Hotel, Buxton, further north in the Peak District, in the early twentieth century*

# MINE HUNTING HOST
## Jack Crook of Devon

For much of his seventy-four years, Jack Crook has lived for horses and hunting. He has also enjoyed more than the odd stirrup cup and there have been many times when the mixing of such interests has produced a cocktail of misfortune. Jack recalls:

'One day I rode over to the Rising Sun and got tanked up on too much Scotch. On the way back I tried to jump this very big fence, but the horse came back on me and I gashed my head. Down at Newton [Abbot] hospital I had to have four stitches, but when I asked for an anaesthetic the doctor said: "I think you've had enough already."

'I also used to go to other boozers in me horse and trap, for a couple of hours from about six in the evening. One night I was over at Kingsteignton with Tony Skedgell when this woman called out to us: "Do you know this is a one-way street?" Tony called back: "Yes, and we're only goin' one way." So she phoned the police and they phoned my wife, Gin. Although that woman who reported us didn't know our names, the police knew there was only one mad bugger about here with a horse and trap.

'One of our local policemen was a bloody nuisance, always comin' round to hide behind the wall by the cellar just as I called time in the bar. So one night I chucked some water over the wall, pretending that I didn't know he was there, and out 'e came in a rush.

'One year I was privileged to lead Newton carnival on my horse, and as I rode through the town this huntin' friend saw me, dashed into the nearby supermarket and came out with a can of beer to keep me going. Then I held the whole procession up while I drank it!'

The son of a horseman and born at Tiverton on 20 September 1924, Jack soon became very interested in most country pursuits. As a boy he worked for Uffculme Co-operative Wholesale Society for a few years before joining the Great Western Railway in 1941, as a footplate fireman. Eventually he qualified as a driver, 'but it was a real case of dead man's shoes unless you were prepared to move away', so in 1967 he took redundancy money and became the tenant of the Heavitree Brewery's Jolly Sailor at East Ogwell, near Newton Abbot. The pub had been neglected for some time.

'I'd known the pub before as I used to come out 'ere helpin' a local farmer with the harvest. They say it got its name from the days when the press gangs used to visit to pick up more labour. There's certainly always been a lot of Navy chaps hereabouts, and we're not too far from the sea. But we never knew how old the building was. Apparently it was two cottages knocked into one in the 1920s – one ol' chap always said 'e was born in our bedroom. The walls were ever so thick, all cob and stone, so they must have gone back a few centuries.

*The publican with his friends at another Devonshire pub, the Setting Sun, Torrington, at the turn of the century*

'When Gin and I went there we wouldn't move into the livin' quarters because it was so filthy, so while the place was done up we stayed in a caravan for seven weeks. Poor Gin – that's an old family name, by the way, and nothing to do with pubs – well, she spent ages cleaning this iron bath which had become black, but when she got to the bottom she discovered it was cracked, so she'd wasted all that time. Then we accidentally dropped some liquid on the floor and discovered that the carpet was not brown after all, but red. I shot rats out the window and discovered loads of others dead under the floorboards. In them days the takin's was only £60 a week, but we soon got up to £150 with new attractions such as a skittle alley in the old pig barn I bought.

'There was a lot of labour about in those days and most of our customers were workers from farms, the council, the waterworks and so on. Some of them were great characters, including Reg Mathews, a poacher known as Greybird who never did a day's work in his life. He was always borrowing a pound and you rarely got your money back.

'Edward Stone was a real boozer. One night, when there was a lot of snow, someone came in and said there was a pair of boots out in the car park. When I went to investigate I discovered there was someone inside the boots – completely buried by the snow! It was Edward Stone, who'd been in such a state that when he slipped he couldn't get up again. And the more he struggled the more he covered himself over. 'E'd 'ave been dead by the morning if his boots hadn't been spotted.

'Then there was Bill Cann who used to get up on the table to sing, but one night 'e forgot 'e was up there and stepped right off with one hell of a bang. He never did get back up after that. Bill Cann and Jeff Thomson each drank ten pints of farm cider a day, so we had no problem in getting through forty gallons every week.

'We always made our own amusement, but now there's just two tellies in our old bar. We used to 'ave a good sing-song most Saturdays, especially with a huntin' crowd in. It was always the tradition with the hunt to finish up in the evenin' where you started off in the mornin', so they'd come back to the pub on days we held meets there – generally two or three times a year each for both the South Devon and the Dart Vale. Luckily we never had any antis in as we had too many supporters around, but there were a few out on the moor I had to put my whip round. The pub meets stopped in about 1987 because the area had become too built up, but we were able to continue with hunt supporters' club meetings.'

Jack started hunting with the South Devon and the Dart Vale in the 1950s, when he was still on the railways. In those days he did not own his own horse but would 'borrow anyone's that needed exercising'. Later he whipped-in to the Dart Vale for three years and not only had his own hunter but also stabled two others. Generally, he hunted three days a fortnight, but insists that his passion did not interfere with the running of the pub.

'I'd never go off without leaving everything completely ready for opening by nine o'clock in the morning. Nowadays they don't know the meaning of the word work –

*Hunting has been a lifetime's interest for Jack (centre)*

you go in many pubs and they're still moppin' up at eleven o'clock. Course, with all the food laid on now it's much more difficult to get time off. Also, now it's hard to find somewhere to play a simple game of darts, euchre or table skittles because they want every table to eat on. But there aren't many landlords can say they've cooked breakfast on a shovel over the fire. This was what us railway chaps always used to do, so one day I had to do it for my customers in the bar.'

Jack no longer rides to hounds, but remains a keen ferreter and roughshooter. And at his East Ogwell home he remains close to both foxes and the Jolly Sailor. He told me: 'I can still see a vixen and four cubs here any night at the moment. I just go over with a few scraps and whistle 'em up on the green. Also, Gin and I still go down the pub for a game of cards two or three mornin's a week, but I'm afraid most of our old friends are gone now and we'm the last of the boozers.'

*The Hunt often met at the Jolly Sailor*

# THE LEPPARD WHO
# CHANGED HIS SPOTS

*Barry Leppard of Kent*

After attending St Edmund's School at Canterbury, Barry Leppard started training
to become a priest, but soon became 'disillusioned' and sought 'sanctuary among
sinners' – pulling pints! But, then, he was a fourth-generation publican, having been
born in his family's Station Hotel, Sidcup, on 14 September 1942; and, most appropriately
for a Leppard, he started work at his father's Spotted Dog, a country pub at Smart's Hill,
near Penshurst. From there he moved but a very short distance to the delightful Chafford
Arms, Fordcombe, near Tunbridge Wells, where he has now been leaseholder for thirty-
one years. It was there that I met him and a group of his enthusiastic regulars, to talk about
the old days over a pint of locally brewed Larkins and a game of dominoes in the 'bread
and butter' public bar. I started by asking Barry if he had ever seen any ghosts.

'Yes! I've spoken to one at the Spotted Dog, which was originally four cottages, built
in 1480, and became an inn in 1520. It has fine weatherboarding, lots of big beams and
an old wisteria growing all round, so it was always creakin' there, and we often used to

say: "Hullo, it's ol' Charley walkin' about again." Then one winter's evening when I came in the back door the phone was ringing and this bloke was standin' there in a raincoat. I said: "Hang on a minute while I answer that," assuming that he'd come in to make a booking, because in those days nobody went in pubs in the late afternoon. But after I'd finished on the phone and turned to face him he'd vanished. There was no way he could have walked past me out the back door without me seeing him, and when I went round lookin' for him all the other doors were locked. It was most unnerving.

'Other people felt this presence, too. Once, when I was runnin' the restaurant at the Spotted Dog, a woman came in and sat down and immediately went white as a sheet. She suddenly got up and declared: "It's no good, I can't sit in this room," and she walked out, never to return.

'As far as I know we don't have a resident ghost inside the Chafford Arms, but there's certainly a village one – I've seen it! One night in the late sixties we'd been to an away darts match and I was just driving into the pub forecourt when I saw her. I said to the lads in the back of my car: "Did you see that?" "Yes," they said, "it was a bride comin' across the road." "But she didn't come out of the church gate," I added.

'Soon after that I was talking to my next-door neighbour, Tony, and he said: "Oh, you've seen her as well, have you?" He told me that it was this bride who'd been left at the altar. Nowadays she comes through the church wall where the path used to be before they built the lychgate, and from there she crosses the road into Tony's house, which used to be a chapel.'

As we reflected on this, Malcolm Slater decided to lighten the mood with one of his pub jokes. 'My sister and brother were on a narrow boat in the Midlands. He said to her: "While I take the boat up on the canal, will you take this jug and try to find some real ale?" So off she went and met this local chap. "Excuse me," she said, "do you know where I can find some real ale?" "Yes," he replied, "you'll find some in the Bison." "Where's that?" she asked. "Just up the way," he said. So off she went, further along the towpath, and came to this area where the locks were. She looked around for the Bison but couldn't see it anywhere, but there was a pub called the Waterman. In she went, and said: "Excuse me, do you know a pub called the Bison?" "No," said the landlord, in his strong Brummy accent, "we're the only pub in the bison" (basin)!'

Not to be outdone, local farmer Basil Sharp, a Chafford Arms customer for over thirty years, chipped in with a few of his 'definitely true' stories.

'This chap called Freddy Squires used to come in here and get so drunk he'd walk into anything on his way back home, so this lad used to go ahead of him and open all the field gates. Also, people sometimes filled his pocket up with stones, and then 'e was bound to fall over.

'There used to be a six o'clock bus came through here and it was called the Cider Express because it stopped at the Rock and all the other pubs along what we called the Drunken Mile. All the lads used to jump on it and go out to 'ave a good ol' cider up, and on the way back they'd stand at the bus stop with this very poor hedge and a steep drop behind. Well, one night, just as the bus stopped, ol' Freddy Squires, who'd 'ad far too much, fell backwards through this 'edge and rolled right down the bank. "Man

*Some of the 'old school' at Barry Leppard's Chafford Arms*

overboard," the others shouted, but they were all too drunk to help, so the bus driver had to climb down and make the rescue!

'Rainbow was another great character used to come in here. One night 'e was so drunk on cider that when 'e went to walk back to Langton Green 'e fell in the pond and drowned.

'Back in my ol' village of Headcorn we had the pub characters, too. They weren't exactly criminals but they'd get up to all sorts, and they were all mild and cider drinkers then 'cos they didn't 'ave enough money for bitter. One bloke there, Lew George, went into the White Horse one night in May and said to someone: "Well, Bill, I've got me runner beans in flower." So Bill says: "You 'aven't got a green'ouse – 'ow d'you do that? I don't believe you." "Right," said Lew, "there's a pint of cider on it." "OK," said Bill, "you bring a bloom down 'ere tomorrow night, to prove it." But when Lew came in 'e brought a couple of bean seeds in self-raising flour! "There you are," 'e said, "beans in flour," and he won 'is pint.

'Then there was Jim Madden, an ex-naval man who worked on the farm and loved to relate stories to tourists in this bar on a Monday night. His favourite was when 'e asked 'is guv'nor if it was all right to go down and shoot a couple of wild ducks on the Medway that night. So 'e did, and two ducks obligingly got up together. Bang! Bang! Down they both came. But 'e didn't 'ave a dog, so 'e waded in with 'is wellin'tons on and picked the birds up. "But," he'd say, "when I came to pull meself out I grabbed hold of what I thought was two tufts of grass, and to my amazement, when I let go of them they was two hares and I'd caught 'old of their ears! And then, when I emptied me wellin'tons I found I'd got four eels as well!" And the way 'e told this always had people roaring with laughter.'

Not to be outdone, Roy Ashby, who was always 'just going', leaned across the table and told me of other impish old pub-goers.

'Ol' Harry Smith was the lengthman who looked after the road along here – there's a picture of 'im up there in the pub's 1939 bowls team. Well, people were always stopping outside and asking him: "Where's this road go to, young man?" and 'e'd say: "It don't go nowhere, it stays just where it is."

'My father was workin' up at Penshurst Place in about 1947, and 'e was a bit of a drinkin' man so 'e often went in the Leicester Arms there. But one afternoon 'e went back to work well under the weather, found a bottle of gin, got into Lord De L'Isle's bed and fell asleep! How 'e got in there I don't know, but when 'e was discovered 'e soon got the sack.'

Then Tony Brown called out from behind the bar with tales of other rogues. 'Old Alf somebody or other used to come in and sell the same lettuces over and over and always got his pint in return. Then there was this chap who was selling and selling this Christmas tree, until one guy went to pick it up and, of course, it wasn't there because everybody else had bought it as well.'

At that point I'd been there quite a while so I thought it prudent to ask Barry what the normal pub hours were. 'What's normal?' he replied, and everyone fell about with laughter. 'Well, if we're all right for time, would you tell me about the pub's history?' I asked.

'It got its licence in 1861 when the nearby Black Lion lost its licence for keeping contraband in the cellar. This was then a Ware's pub, before Flowers and then Whitbreads, who charged me just £2 a week rent when I came here in the sixties – now it's over £40,000 a year!

'Our sign shows a man leading a packhorse over water and it's taken me over twenty-five years to find out why. I used to go round looking for a Lord Chafford, but couldn't find one, and then I discovered that the area just up the road by the bridge is known as Chafford and there used to be a ford there. Then a customer told me that "cha" is a very old word for a bend in the river – hence chafford for a ford by a bend in the river.

'Then the brewery decided to change the sign and put up a man leading a donkey, with a lot of tinkers and so on. So I got a petition up and put the local paper onto it. Some people said I'd never get the brewery to change their mind, but in the end we won – we beat Whitbreads! After so long in the business you learn how to drive 'em and start to get it right. Mind you, there's been times when our family's got it wrong. Just look at that framed bill over there on the wall. That was when my grandad kept the Old Brewery Tap at Plumstead and was charged with running a betting shop in the pub. They couldn't prove it, but how can you find someone not guilty and charge costs against him like that?'

When you look around the Chafford Arms, the involvement in cricket and other sports is very obvious through photos and other mementoes. Much of this stems from the Leppard family's interests and achievements. Barry himself was once in the British water-skiing team and he still runs a shooting syndicate on land adjacent to the Spotted Dog. But a much more unusual activity propelled Barry to fame.

'About twenty years ago one of my customers brought a skateboard back from New Zealand and I used to get on it out in the road here when it was closed through subsidence. After a while I became quite good at it. Then one day, when I jumped off, my dog jumped on and somebody spotted it. The next thing I knew the media got hold of it and the story was blown right up. They asked if my dog did anything else and I said: "Yes, she's a working gundog," so then the TV people wanted to film her.

'As luck would have it, we were in the shooting season and I had this cock pheasant hanging up, so I told the film crew that when they came down I'd get my dog to retrieve it. Unfortunately, it had been in cold store and, as you know, dogs won't retrieve cold game much. But we had a go and when the cameras were rollin' this chap threw the bird over the hedge while I threw my gun up – bang, bang! My poor old bitch worked that ditch thirteen times before they cut.

'Anyway, all this made a twenty-minute slot on the Nationwide television programme. Now

*Barry's skateboarding dog attracted many customers over the years!*

that's a lot of advertising and the skateboarding dog was a major attraction: over the next number of years literally thousands of people turned up here to see it. Even this year one little ol' lady came in the pub and said: "I believe you have a skateboarding dog." '

Now Barry has turned his skateboard in and he channels his customers towards less vigorous games and pastimes, such as shove-ha'penny, quiz nights, vegetable competitions and dominoes, though the old steel quoits bed in the garden is no longer used.

Other folk have been drawn to Barry's pub for a whole variety of reasons. Some want to reminisce, such as the old chap who came in about fifteen or twenty years ago and said: 'That's where our Home Guard unit 'ad our Bren gun, in the saloon bar window.' When Barry asked him what it was for, he replied: 'Guardin' the crossroads against the Germans. It looked like the best place to me, with a good field of fire.'

Many people have been attracted by the pub's grounds, which won the brewery's

'Garden in Bloom' competition. The garden is charming, with lots of shady bowers and attractive features such as an old, overgrown cider press which Barry brought over from Chiddingstone Heath, and the 1812-pattern Admiralty anchor which he recovered from Rye Harbour. The place is rich in wildlife, too, with some half-dozen foxes and five or six badgers which come every night to feed on the scraps that Barry saves from the kitchen and customers' plates. These mammals have become quite bold, and lucky visitors may see them rooting around under the spotlight very close to the building.

The garden did suffer back in October 1987, as much of Kent took the full force of what has become known as the Great Storm. Barry recalled: 'I had this great big wych elm and when I went out and stood on its roots I went up and down about four inches, so I soon jumped off.'

All this excitement obviously proved too much for Barry's first wife, who left 'when she got fed up with running pubs'. But now he is happily re-married and the pub goes from strength to strength, which is not surprising as his second wife was already a Leppard before she met him!

*Rivalry among the customers at one of the Chafford Arms vegetable competitions*

# FROM DEBAUCHERY
# TO POETRY
*The King's Head Inn, Llandovery, Carmarthenshire*

Few pubs have undergone a more dramatic change of image than the King's Head Inn, in the market town of Llandovery, Carmarthenshire. Centuries of debauchery promptly came to an end in 1971, when David and June Madeira-Cole set about establishing a place 'where nice women do not feel threatened coming in on their own'.

The fabric of the King's Head dates back to the late eleventh century, when Llandovery was occupied by the Normans. Originally a single-storey building, it is thought to have served ale as early as the twelfth century. A town record of 1299 mentions income from 'tolcestre', a tax on the brewing of ale, and the borough charter of 1485 forbade the opening of any tavern in the lordship of Llandovery except in the town itself. It is likely that the King's Head functioned as an inn throughout those early centuries.

The top two floors were added during the reign of Charles I, when the townsfolk sided against Cromwell, and ever since then the King's head has adorned the inn sign. Formerly a separate building, the east-facing section of the inn was the original premises of the Banc yr Eidion Du (Bank of the Black Ox), founded in 1799 by David Jones, a drover anxious to avoid carrying large amounts of cash while moving Welsh black cattle to England, thereby avoiding highway robbery. This was one of the most successful of Welsh private banks and remained there until the early 1900s, when the business moved, allowing the premises to become part of one of the most popular coaching inns in the area. In 1909 the Jones bank was sold to Lloyds. Papers pertaining to the business, including fragments of bank notes, are still displayed at the King's Head. Some of these were found sandwiched between the lath and plaster walls during renovations in 1972.

On the south-east corner of the inn is a very old stone which was positioned to protect the building from damage by cart wheels. Much later, in the reign of George II, it provided further security as well as a place to gain attention when Howell Harris stood on it to preach to hostile crowds.

In this century many auctions, sales and functions have been held in the pub's 'Long Room', which served as a soup kitchen and a social club for local ladies during World War II. It was also used to entertain prisoners of war who were detained in camps on the edge of town, as well as British troops stationed at Sennybridge. But it is chiefly Llandovery's position, at the head of the farming valley of the River Towy and on ancient trading routes, that is behind the prosperity of both the town and the King's Head.

The drovers who converged on Llandovery from time immemorial, probably reaching their greatest numbers in the nineteenth century, were a rowdy, rough-living and hard-drinking lot. They may have spent a lot of money, but they also generated great intemperance and lewdness at hostelries such as the King's Head, a tradition which continued into modern times, as June Madeira-Cole explained.

'After their long, hard treks along remote tracks, these men were keen to have a good time and would often get so drunk they'd bust the place up. Also, the market square, where we are, was always the pick-up point where prospective drovers and farm workers stood each morning hoping to be hired; and it was common for fighting to break out among those wishing to shorten the odds. The tradition of the market square as the pick-up point continues today: every morning builders, carpenters, electricians and plumbers stop off to collect their workforce. Fortunately, most of them are well behaved.

'In order to encourage trade, in the old days all bed-and-breakfast places here were required by law to provide ale, so there were over a hundred licensed premises in the town. There were still about sixty-seven of these in the 1940s, before the sudden decline of droving – brought about chiefly by the great expansion and improvement of rail and road transport.

'When we came here the town still had twenty-one pubs, of which we were the only free house. Now there are fourteen and only two of these are brewery-owned. But even this number is large for a place with only 1,600 people on the electoral roll.

'We bought the pub with our hearts, not our heads, as the King's Head was extremely run down. The mayor quickly came round to see us, even before we'd completed the purchase, and we thought he'd kindly come to welcome us, but instead he served us with a dangerous structure notice! It turned out that part of the front wall was likely to fall out and we had to spend a lot more money to put things right.

*Seconds later this 'reveller' fell off the bench – the result of one pint too many!*

'We also discovered that the King's Head still had a very bad reputation as a raucous centre for drugs and drunkenness, and apparently some of the girls who had been serving there were also accustomed to providing "services of a personal nature". The place still had paintings of dancing girls on the walls.'

At the same time, Liverpool-born June and Lancashire lad David, who had previously managed his family's hotel, were certainly not averse to good clean fun. Indeed, when Carmarthenshire was still one of the Welsh counties that was 'dry' on a Sunday, they sometimes accompanied Llandovery townsfolk on a hired coach for an evening booze-up in nearby 'wet' Breconshire, even though June has never been much of a drinker. But that was only when the King's Head had no guests to look after. As June said, 'We could always serve residents and their guests at any time, and "guests" could cover a multitude of sins, but you had to be careful in case of a spy.'

While rejecting 'new-fangled things such as TV, juke-box, pin-ball machines and one-armed bandits, as well as hooligans and nasty drunks', June and David encouraged more peaceful activities such as monthly farmers' meetings and performances by choirs. Furthermore, David is renowned for his excellent poetry, much of it about the pub and its customers and written in a book snappily entitled *Thoughts Behind Bars*. He generally has the courage to show it to the people he writes about, and some pieces have been published in anthologies and magazines. One of my favourites is reproduced here:

### THE PROFESSIONAL SILLY ASS

Peregrine couldn't spell his own name,
but at a very early age
he learned to say 'Good health!'
and 'Jolly good show',
and opened doors for ladies
so they could go.

His manners were impeccable,
his tailor irreplaceable.
From the time he was weaned
he kept his nose clean
but still didn't know
how to spell his own name.

Quite a dandy, quite a card,
debutantes wanted him in their back yard.
At parties he's been a great success
but his career is in a mess
because he still can't spell his name.

Unlike many of their predecessors at the King's Head, the Madeira-Coles have reached the heights of respectability, with June on the town council and so on, yet their reign has not been without colourful subjects. One of the most lively was a circuit judge who stayed regularly, would only ever eat June's shepherd's pie and beans and drank almost a whole bottle of gin every night.

When I spoke to the Madeira-Coles, David was in long-term ill-health and they were understandably looking forward to retirement, but their only son was unable to take on the pub. Let us hope that their successor is as successful as they have been at blending the best of old and new.

# PERSISTENT AS THEY COME

*Noreen Haswell of Tyneside and Pembrokeshire*

Few people have been more single-minded than Noreen Haswell (née Nolan) in achieving their ambition to run a successful country pub. And what a task she set herself! Not only did she start applying to breweries as a single woman, in the days when virtually all new licences were given to men (and few women went into pubs alone), but also she decided to settle in Wales when she did not know a word of Welsh.

Born at Heaton, Newcastle-on-Tyne, on 25 July 1923, Noreen left school in 1939, in the same year that her father died. She worked as a secretary before joining the WRAC in 1950. After training she was posted to Manorbier in Pembrokeshire, and then to Anglesey, and finally to the War Office in London. Then Noreen returned home to Tyneside and resumed secretarial work until she could achieve her ambition to run a country pub.

'Mother ran a shop in North Shields, where she had a beer licence as well as selling everything from groceries to haberdashery, so I knew a little about the drinks trade. And my original idea was that Mother would sell up and help me in a pub.

'The first thing I did was to go to my local library and read the *Brewers' Manual* to find out who owned most of the pubs in Pembrokeshire, which I'd got to love while in the Army, and I knew that most of the pubs there were small enough for me to cope with. But I also realised that as a single woman I wouldn't stand a chance of being accepted, so when I applied I simply signed myself N.C. Nolan.

'My first response was from Ansells and when they asked me down for interview they suggested that I brought my wife! I think they had a bit of a shock when I wrote admitting the truth, but they were very good to me, and while they said that it wasn't their policy to offer pubs to single women they would find me a job as a trainee manager. But that was no good to me as I wanted my own pub to inject my personality into.

'Then I went for interview with Simmonds of Reading, a nice little family firm, and they had a surprise when a young woman walked through the door. This very polite gentleman listened sympathetically to my story about why I wanted Pembrokeshire and then told me that they didn't own any pubs there. "But I've seen your beer down there," I said. "That's right," he replied, "but we sell it through an agent – James Williams of Narberth, Pembrokeshire. Maybe they can help you as they own some small pubs like you're looking for. I'll ring them for you."

'Well, I went away thinking that would be the last I'd hear of that, but I was wrong and very soon I was invited down for interview by James Williams. There I met this very autocratic type who said that he had a small place I could run. It was the Hope in Pembroke, a tiny pub, but I knew it well and it was very successful. However, the previous tenant had had a heart attack and they wanted a replacement for him within three weeks. But we couldn't go there that quickly as Mother had a business to sell, and I didn't quite have the confidence to go it alone then, so I turned it down.

'After that I went to help a friend who was widowed at twenty-nine and whose husband had left her nineteen pubs. She decided to sell eighteen of them and invest a lot of money in the one remaining, a very famous Tynemouth pub called the Gibraltar Rock. I went there for about six months, until my friend sold out to Flowers, and I learnt a lot about beer and accounts, and so on; but every pub and every area has its own character so I couldn't really learn anything that would help me in Pembrokeshire.

'While I was at the Gibraltar Rock I met Tom and we married the same year. I wrote to James Williams again and they asked me to bring Tom down for interview! They obviously liked him and before long they offered me another pub. Although it meant breaking our honeymoon in Scotland, we went to look at it straight away – the St Brides Inn at Little Haven, which is one of the prettiest coastal villages in west Wales. It was a lovely old place, but the couple in it put us off. The man said we'd never take much money there because everyone locally was intermarried and that his wife's mother already had all the trade in the district at the Swan. But his story didn't make sense because then he said that sometimes they'd been so inundated with tourists wanting to stay he'd even had to give up his bed and sleep in the bath! And when we asked to see the cellar he just opened these two doors and there was all the beer set into a recess in the rock face. It was beautifully cold for the beer but the place was running with water – slime really. Hygienically you wouldn't get away with that nowadays. Also, the pub was right down in a cleft between the cliffs and the buses never went down there

*A stirrup cup outside the Llwyngwair Arms prior to 'beating the bounds' in 1973. Pictured with Newport Mayor Clayton Thatcher is Welsh writer and broadcaster Wynford Vaughan Thomas, a pub regular who had a holiday cottage nearby*

because they couldn't turn, so my mother would have had to walk all the way up the steep hill every time she wanted to catch one, and we didn't have a car. So taking all these things together we decided that this pub, too, wasn't right for us.

'After that James Williams offered us another pub, in Neyland, but that was in an industrial area near Milford Haven so I said no. Then we were offered what was considered to be one of Williams' better pubs, the Llwyngwair Arms at the coastal village of Newport, and fortunately we liked it because it was inferred that if we turned it down there wouldn't be any more chances after wasting so much of the owners' time.

'I had been worried because I couldn't speak any Welsh, especially as Newport was above what they call the Landsker Line, an imaginary line which for 800 years has divided Pembrokeshire in half, between the native Celtic stronghold to the north and the Norman-settled south, which is often referred to as "Little England Beyond Wales". But when I spoke about this to the head of James Williams, he said: "Don't worry about that – they can all speak English if they want to." Even so, in 1958 when we moved in, we didn't hear a word of English for two days! The local people clearly missed the couple who were there before us, George and Barbara Scarr.

'We had other problems, too. Mother couldn't come for three months as her shop sale had yet to be finalised, which meant we didn't have any furniture or anything else much for the home, so we had to buy two mattresses and sleep on the floor. Apart from that we started with just a few cups and saucers and a frying pan and a couple of chairs and a table which the Scarrs had loaned us.

'George Scarr went away to sea and Barbara Scarr put all her belongings in store. She said that she was going to devote the summer to her children as she'd neglected them so much through the pub, so she took a caravan up on the mountain behind us and intended to go house-hunting in the winter. But disaster struck. Just three weeks after they moved she put the two children to bed and went to a nearby friend's to get milk. While she was gone the caravan caught fire and the children were suffocated and died.

'This made us even more unpopular as the locals had loved that family. And our phone never stopped ringing as reporters latched on to the story, especially with the husband going away and leaving the family to cope. Just about the whole of Newport turned out for the Scarr children's funeral, but hardly anyone came in the pub. Our takings were only about £50 in the first week, in late May, and they continued to be low. On top of all this I was several months pregnant and certainly not in the right frame of mind to cope.

'About a week after the funeral I told Tom that I couldn't stand it any more – we'd have to go. So he said: "Yes, if it doesn't improve after another week or two you'd better go back home and decide what to do." But then, on 27 June, the fun fair came for its annual visit, and although the people who ran it had known the Scarrs the loss of the children didn't mean the same to them. So they pulled the curtains back and started to dance and laugh. They really saved the day, and from then on everything changed. Even so, it still took us five years to become fully accepted.

'We soon discovered that you can't organise the Welsh, but nevertheless I get on very well with them. They are wonderful people in emergencies or trouble. There's a lot of individuality in the villages, especially among the old people. We had a lot of great characters among our customers and Tom often sketched them. There was J.O. Vaughan, the farmer and alderman, who was the first person in Newport to have a car yet he was still driving to the pub when we came here. Then there was the farm labourer Dai Hebert, who was very cute at bar skittles. He was very Welsh and when English

*Among the customers sketched by Tom Haswell were alderman J.O. Vaughan (right), the first man in Newport to own a car, and (opposite) Dai Herbert, who won many a pint through his skill at skittles*

tourists came in he pretended to know little about the game, but when he played the visitors for a glass of beer he always won!

'Another regular was a retired carpenter called Dai, who was very methodical and set in his ways. He always arrived punctually just a few minutes before evening opening time and stood outside looking at his grandfather's old fob watch. Now this was a bit irritating for us, so one day Tom said to me: "I'll fix the old so-and-so." At the time tape recorders were just becoming popular and Tom had been given one as part of a promotion, so he recorded the six o'clock pips and news then hid the machine beneath the bar.

'Next evening Tom delayed opening for a few minutes, so when Dai entered he chastised Tom: "You're late, boy!" Then Tom secretly switched on the tape recording and said: "No, Dai, I'm on time. Listen – there's the six o'clock pips going now." Dai stared in disbelief at his faithful old watch and said: "Aye, aye; I never ever thought you'd let me down." But it was painful to see his dismay, so Tom felt obliged to confess.

'One day when I had just coped with an awkward order for drinks this customer insisted that I had a drink for myself, on him. Then Alwyn the butcher, who shared Tom's great sense of fun, remarked: "Strange thing, business; when I've dealt with a difficult order no one ever says to me, "Now take a chop for yourself." At that there was a great roar of laughter.

'One winter we had a sudden blizzard and our bank manager, who lived in Cardigan, was trapped here, so we offered to put him up. He could walk to the bank from us and he really enjoyed being looked after so well and coming down in the evening for a pint and a game of darts with the boys. We were entirely cut off by the snow for three days, but the farmers could use their tractors and gradually cleared a narrow road from Newport as far as the Llwyngwair Manor. Then a few of the locals suggested a run over there and they took the bank manager with them. Imagine his surprise and embarrass-ment when he discovered several folk he knew from Cardigan town already there. The road from Cardigan to the Manor had been cleared by the council with the aid of farm-ers, so his wife could well have been suspicious about the fact that he hadn't driven home earlier! But you must remember that the phones were out of action because the old overhead wires were down.

'Another cold time, the Newport choir were going to give a concert in the local hall on St David's Day, but during the afternoon it snowed so hard the organisers spent a couple of hours in our pub debating whether or not to cancel the event. After many pints they decided that they would, but unfortunately a local lady had already sent in her regular newspaper column of Newport news, anticipating that the concert would go ahead. She made the whole thing up, even saying how wonderful the choir was and detailing what they'd sung, and when this appeared in two papers there were some very red faces around.'

Many years ago the Llwyngwair Arms used to be owned by the big local landowners, the Bowens, whose mansion was turned into the Llwyngwair Manor Hotel. They used to collect their tenants' rents in our big room upstairs and the council collected rents in what is now the gents' toilet. Also in the big room we used to run all sorts of educational things, such as art and literature appreciation, organised by the extramural department of Aberystwyth University. But Tuesday was always kept free for farming things as we served a very rural community. We also provided a punch stirrup cup when the Tivy-Side Hunt met here.

'One ancient ceremony that's still held in the big room is the annual Court Leet, when the burgesses and aldermen select the mayor, on the same day that the Lord Mayor of London is chosen. The Court Leet administers the common grazing land on the hill above – each person whose property abuts the common having the right to graze three sheep or one horse or one cow there. Once a year the Court Leet aldermen and some of the burgesses meet at the pub to arrange the ancient ceremony of beating of the bounds, when local children and visitors are encouraged to walk the parish boundaries. Years ago the children were symbolically beaten on these boundaries, then given sweets so that they never forgot the boundary sitings.

'Newport's market charter dates from 1278 and when the market stopped this led to a few problems in the pubs. When we came here as a couple of rookies from the north-east of England they were open all day on Friday, and when I asked why, they said: "Oh, it's market day." "But there isn't any market," I said, "it finished years ago." What happened was that the farmers still traditionally came in on Friday to bring their wives shopping while they caught up on all the news and conducted business with people such as seed merchants and insurance agents, who knew that they'd still be around. And, of course, most of their meetings took place in the pubs.

'All-day opening continued to be linked with markets in other towns and villages, too, whether they had a market or not, and as these were held on different days anyone clever could get a drink somewhere in the area at almost any time of day on six days a week. But as cars came in more, and people could travel around more easily, this started to get out of hand so the police decided something had to be done about it.

'The chief constable was sent down to sort it all out, and as Newport didn't even have a market any more we were the prime target and they started to prosecute people. On one occasion in 1960 eighty-three-year-old J.O. Vaughan, eighty-two-year-old John Evans and sixty-five-year-old John Davies were fined 20s each 'for consuming intoxicating liquor at the Golden Lion, Newport, during non-permitted hours', despite their pleas that they thought it was market day. Licensee Harold Griffiths was also fined – 20s on each of the three summonses. PC Halcourt Jones had caught the men when he called in the pub at 4.55pm.

'For two or three years the argument continued, and as we used the old excuse that the farmers still needed an occasion to meet we won the day when the issue was first raised at the brewster sessions [regulating authority for the drinks trade]. Our hours then were 11.30am to 3pm and 6 to 10pm Monday to Saturday, but 11.30am right through to 10pm on Friday. Then, in the early 1960s, new laws allowed another hour a day so we decided to open at 11am to try to catch the holidaymakers before they went down on the beach, and in the evening at 5.30. Also, we used to apply for an extension to 10.30pm on Fridays and Saturdays in July and August to accommodate the farm workers and their dependants, who were tied to working long hours while the daylight lasted. Of course, you could serve anyone during that extra time, but in those days there weren't many visitors as the area was still too remote for most people. Later we got an extension for farm workers in June, too, and when tourism started to take off we were allowed to stay open to 11pm from June to August. Then in one year the usual August Bank Holiday happened to be in September so, as that day was so important for trade, they allowed the extension in that month, too.

'The other big thing was Sunday opening. When we started, no Welsh pubs were open on that day and we loved it as we had a whole day to ourselves. Also, there was very little tourism for us to cash in on then, and the local people only had a certain amount of money to

*One of Noreen's most surprising pub curios. It must have been a very special umbrella to warrant the printing of two dozen such posters*

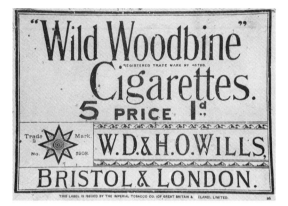

*This large 'Wild Woodbine' cigarette box is one of Noreen's oldest mementoes from the Llwyngwair Arms*

spend. If it was gone on Saturday they certainly wouldn't come in on Sunday. Being dominated by agriculture, wages were generally very low at Newport and we often had people asking for the loan of a fiver – even a 10 shilling note. And you'd often lose this or it would be ages before they paid you back, because there were three other pubs there and the people would play you off against each other. While they still owed you money they'd drink at the other places.

'Mind you, although there wasn't much money about we did remarkably well with fruit machines. When we first put one in the locals were amazed as they'd never seen anything like it. We had to split the money three ways, with the pub owners and the machine operators, but even so in the first few weeks we took almost as much as we did from bar profits! We were worried that this wouldn't last and that we'd get to rely on it, so we decided to invest the money in the business, in getting a local man to make new window shutters, which are still up.

'Also there were other reasons for opposing the Sunday opening. One chap who loved his pint said to me: "You won't be seeing me on a Sunday evening. I've always lived routinely and Sunday is our family day, when we do everything together."

'But I suppose change was inevitable, and the first time we had the county voting for Sunday opening there was a big surprise. When the Licensed Victuallers' Association secretary came round all the pubs we told him that he wouldn't have much support in the north as most people were very chapel-minded there. Only a handful of youngsters would want the pubs open, mostly those who had been away to work or be educated. So he said to me: "Well, Mrs Haswell, it doesn't matter very much because in the south of the county all those tourist places such as Tenby, Saundersfoot and Pembroke Dock, with bigger populations, they'll vote yes and the north is going to be absolutely outvoted." There was even a special beer mat – "Say YES to Sunday opening" – printed by the National Licensed Victuallers' Association in collaboration with the Brewers' Society.

'Anyhow, when voting day came along there was a very poor turnout of only 25–30% in the big-population areas in the south, but in the north there was a huge turnout. For example, Newport had about 70% and Moylegrove, which didn't even have a pub within miles, recorded 86%, most of whom said no. To help achieve this, the ministers had worked really hard, flying back and forth in their cars. As a result, it was the north that really swamped the south.

'However, the next time the issue was raised, after the mandatory further seven years, the LVA pulled all their big guns out and won the day, in the early 1960s. I had a big map of Wales on the wall and as the results came through I coloured in all the counties accordingly. This made clear that it was all the pubs which bordered England – right down the marches – which were in favour of change, while virtually all those away in the west said no. But when the next seven-year vote came round the yes vote spread like a wave from east to west because customers were starting to travel much more to drink and pubs were forced to compete with their neighbours.

'James Williams, who were founded in 1830 and still operate about fifty pubs in Pembrokeshire and Carmarthenshire, gave up brewing beer themselves but were wonderful bottlers. They used to bring Guinness in from Ireland and my mother was a great Guinness drinker so one day Tom said, "Let's play a trick on her." Well, there was this other landlady nearby and we often used to borrow crates of drink from each other when we ran out. One day she had a crate of Guinness from us, but she replaced it with some brewed in London and bottled by Watneys rather than James Williams. So when Mother came down as usual at about half past nine to wash a few glasses up and serve if we were busy, we gave her one of these Watneys bottles. And she would never do anything without her Guinness first. But as soon as she tasted it she said: "There's something wrong with it." And at that all the customers roared with laughter as they knew what was going on. It just went to show how much a bottle of drink could vary then. We had a tremendous sale for our Dublin-brewed and Williams-bottled Guinness.

'My husband was always dead against pubs turning into glorified restaurants so we generally only did food to special order. But sometimes people got us mixed up with the Llwyngwair Manor Hotel, which was a smart place and did lots of food, because we came before them in the telephone directory. Mistakenly, we often received phone calls meant for them. Well, one day these BBC people did this and telephoned from Cardiff to book lunch for six. I asked if something simple would do and they said yes, so as I was a good pastry cook I decided to make a big steak-and-mushroom pie, which would also be easy to get ready quickly. Unfortunately, the group didn't turn up so I was left with this huge pie, and I'd been very generous with the meat. Also, we couldn't eat it up ourselves as I'd made one for the family at the same time. So I decided to make some pasties with it and I put them out on the bar counter. Well, they sold like hot cakes, and after that people started asking for more so I made them regularly on a Friday and Saturday. And this was a very good thing for our trade generally because wives would say to their husbands: "If you're going for a drink you might as well call in at the Llwyngwair and get four pasties," or whatever. And I'd put them on top of the Rayburn so that they were nice and warm for the men to take home at the end of the evening. But after about three years of this it started to get out of hand, with holidaymakers knocking on the door at ten in the morning to ask for a dozen pasties at a time, when all my domestic cooker could cope with was nine in one batch. So, reluctantly, I gave it up.'

In 1975 the Haswells left the Llwyngwair Arms in order to give their daughter 'a bit more of home life', so they bought a nearby house and Tom returned to engineering, to work for Sealink, while Noreen studied for a teaching diploma. But in 1981 they returned to the trade, taking a pub in the county town of Haverfordwest, where the business was far less seasonal than it had been at Newport.

Finally, in 1985 they moved to a pub called The Pump on the Green, at the nearby prosperous village of Spittal, where they remained until retirement in 1991. As Noreen recalls, 'It was a place always full of laughter. It was the village's first pub and only about twenty years old, having been created from an old shop with a petrol pump outside. A lot of our customers were young farmers who used to tease my husband terribly. They were always bringing him posters, ash trays, pot plants and other things from different pubs, and it got so out of hand we were worried that people might think we were encouraging them.

'We also had a lot of singing back at the Llwyngwair, with the choir in regularly, which was good for business as they generated a marvellous atmosphere. The only trouble was that when they got going it was difficult to get them and everybody else out because they thought that if they kept on they'd be able to get another round in at a quarter past eleven or so.'

Shortly after the Haswells bought their Newport house, Tom happened to see that his old cocktail bar at the Llwyngwair had been put out with the rubbish, so he asked if he could have it. This was duly installed in the Haswell house and became Tom's pride and joy. 'He even put shelving up on the walls around it, and covered them with bottles,' Noreen told me. But sadly Tom did not have too much time to enjoy his 'toy' as he died in 1993, just two years after retiring, and then the bar had to go to make more space for Noreen's newly married daughter and son-in-law. Even so, the house remained crammed with mementoes of Noreen's dedication to pubs, with objects ranging from probably the first Woodbine cigarette box ever made to a plaque presented to the couple by the draymen. She even has copies of all the letters she wrote to the breweries when she was hunting for her first pub back in the 1950s!

# SIGNS OF THE TIMES
## Our Earliest Pub Signs

In ancient times, when few people could read, let alone write, it was important for any business or trade to display an easily understood and easily remembered token or sign. While most of these have largely disappeared as illiteracy has become the exception rather than the rule, inn signs remain widespread as a wonderful tradition and link with our rich heritage.

Signs for public houses, inns, taverns and alehouses – call them what you will – have European origins going back at least 2,000 years, to Pompeii and Herculaneum, when a board showing two slaves carrying a wine skin marked the door of a wine merchant. In ancient Rome vine leaves generally symbolised Bacchus, the god of wine, and were displayed outside wine outlets, called tabernae, from which the term 'tavern' derived – a place in which native Britons could enjoy their preferred ale.

Our ancestors also adopted the Roman tradition of a sign, the earliest of which were called ale-stakes. However, vines were rare in Roman-occupied Britain so the poles would generally be hung with a clump of ivy or other evergreens rather than vine leaves, to signify a tavern selling both wine and ale. Not surprisingly, then, later painted signs often featured bushes and today we still have many pubs bearing names such as the Holly Bush.

*(above) This remarkable sign at The White Hart, Scole, Norfolk, is said to have cost over £1,000 in Tudor times. This engraving is from 1825, but sadly the sign no longer exists*

Another ancient sign used to distinguish public houses was the red lattice. Whether to provide ventilation or because glass was too expensive, early alehouse windows were generally left open, as were those of many cottages. Therefore to give customers some privacy and the owners some security, a lattice, grille or trellis was placed across the window space. This grille was usually painted red and this became so common that almost every tavern could be distinguished by it. Indeed, in Elizabethan times there were so many that the dramatist Dekker commented: 'A whole street is in some places but a continuous alehouse, not a shop to be seen between red lattice and red lattice.' Although these have long since disappeared their use has been commemorated in some corrupted inn names, such as The Green Lettuce.

Another sign which is generally thought to go back further than the Middle Ages is The Chequers, which remains fairly common today throughout the country. Certainly wine shops in ancient Pompeii were distinguished by it, and chess was a popular game in Roman taverns. No doubt the Romans brought this custom to Britain, when they invaded us and set up alehouses for their thirsty legions.

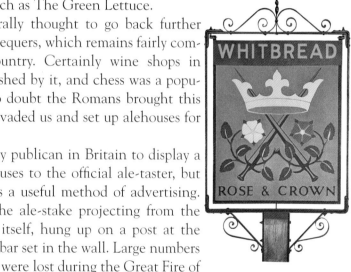

In 1393 a law compelled every publican in Britain to display a sign, primarily to identify alehouses to the official ale-taster, but they soon became recognised as a useful method of advertising. Such signs could be fixed on the ale-stake projecting from the building, carved on the façade itself, hung up on a post at the front, or suspended from an iron bar set in the wall. Large numbers were lost during the Great Fire of London, after which many more signs were carved in the stonework of new buildings, and then painted or gilded.

As the number of taverns grew along with the population, tavern keepers had to be more inventive with their names and signs, to distinguish them from the

*(top left) This panel sign (now in the Victoria & Albert Museum) from The White Hart, Witley, Surrey, was re-painted in 1875 by famous artists Birket Foster and Alfred Cooper. The White Hart, now owned by Shepherd Neame (England's oldest independent brewery, established in 1698), was Foster's local and is said to have Britain's longest continuous licence, dating back to the fourteenth century; (centre) 1938 sign for the Rose & Crown, Seal, Kent, among so many which have their origins in loyalty to the monarch; (left) innumerable pub signs have sporting associations. This 1947 example is from North Finchley*

*The sign speaks for itself: the Crown Inn at Chiddingfold, Surrey*

mass. Many had religious themes, such as Ye Olde Trip to Jerusalem, commemorating the Crusades, on what is now one of our oldest surviving pubs, in Nottingham. Others wanted to show allegiance to the king, through names such as The King's Head or Rose & Crown, or to Catholicism through The Pope's Head, The Angel, and so on. The variety and reasons were endless.

While illiteracy remained rife many names became corrupt. For example, The Swan with Two Necks actually derived from the system of marking the 'royal' swans with two nicks. In the end many of the names became so obscure there was public outcry. In 1710 the *Spectator* magazine called for a government official to control the more ludicrous.

At the same time signs became bigger and more extravagant. One of the most elaborate was that of The White Hart at Scole, Norfolk, which developed into triumphal arches spanning the road above the traffic. The twenty-five life-sized figures in black oak which composed the sign are said to have cost over a thousand pounds, an enormous sum in Tudor times.

Eventually there were many complaints about such large signs obstructing the light and air, so attempts were made to regulate them. At one time in the fifteenth century the ale-stake was limited to 7ft high, under a penalty of £40 – a huge fine when best ale was only three ha'pence a gallon! Another law, in Charles II's reign, forbade signs that projected the width of the roadway, and in 1718 a sign in Bride Lane, Fleet Street, was so heavy it caused the front of the tavern to collapse on four passers-by! Let us hope that they were drunk enough not to feel the pain.

# ACKNOWLEDGEMENTS

I am especially indebted to all the people who are the subjects of this book, and their relatives, for their great kindness and hospitality.

For advice and leads I would specially like to thank the following individuals, organisations and publications: Cath Allen, Allied Brewery Traders Association, Derek Andrews, Roy Ashby, David Barton, British Institute of Innkeeping, Tony Brown, William Cheeseman, Noreen Clark, Edward Connolly, John Dodd, Jol Foster, David Geering, Tom Halpin (brewery historian and food science consultant), Chris Harris, Shelley Jeffrey, Tony Newman, June O'Neill, Andrew Prowse, Publican Magazine, Tom Quinn of The Countryman magazine, Mr T. M. Reid of the London & South-East Licensed Victuallers Association, Henry Scott, Basil Sharp, Tony Sherwood, Tony Short, Bernard Shough, Clive Smith of The Licensee and Morning Advertiser, Malcolm Slater, Bruce Watt and Les Woodland.

Of the many breweries and pub-owning companies contacted, my particular thanks go to Mr B. Segrave-Daly of Adnams, Bass Taverns, Matthew Batham of Daniel Batham & Son, Belhaven, Mr R. C. May-Hill of S. A. Brain, Century Inns, Mr D. Agnew of Discovery Inns, Mr T. Stork of Elgood & Son, Mr H. Constantine-Cort of Enville Ales, Felinfoel, Mike Perry of Flowers, Sophie Knight of Fuller's, Mr N. Atkinson of George Gale, David King of Gibbs Mew, Mr T. Bridge, Frances Brace and Rona Critchley at Greene King, Audrey Lloyd-Kitchen of Greenalls, David Woodhouse and Mr N. J. Sellick of Hall and Woodhouse, Mr R. Hanson of Hardys & Hansons, Mr L. Wood of Heavitree, Jonathan Holden of Holden's, Mr P. Hyde of Hydes Anvil, David Mallard of King & Barnes, Mr W. G. R. Lees-Jones of J. W. Lees, Mansfield, Sue Shakespeare at Marston's, Peter Morland of Morland's, Wilma Johnstone of Morrells, Murphy, Mr A. J. C. Palmer of Palmer's, Pheonix Inns, Christopher Pope of Eldridge Pope, Redruth, David Welsh of Ringwood Brewery, Mr D. Robinson of Frederic Robinson, St Austell, John Fleming of T. & R. Theakston, Daniel Thwaites, Mr C. Dent of Timothy Taylor, Mr R. A. Stafford of Ushers, Frank Nicholson of Vaux, Jonathan Pollock of Wadsworth's, M. J. Robinson and other staff at Whitbreads, and James Williams.

Finally, special thanks to my patient editor, Sue Hall; and to my wife Carol for her help and encouragement.

The author and publishers would like to thank the following for providing photographs:

Beaford Archive pp 1, 7, 8, 15, 24, 163 and 175; Getty Images pp 3, 73, 95, 127, 137, 144, 154 and 188; Hardys & Hansons pp 4, 12, 112, 113 and 160–1; The Bass Museum pp 9, 10, 11, 141 and 142; *The Countryman* magazine p17; John Cleare/Mountain Camera p20; Greene King pp 31, 32 and 157; Derek Croucher pp 33, 69, 75, 102, and 167; Eldridge Pope pp 37 and 108; Associated Newspapers p53; Express & Echo pp 64 and 67; R.F. Bevan p 146 and West of England Newspapers p165

Colour artworks by Michael Lye except pages 65 and 156 by John Paley

# INDEX

(Page numbers in *italics* indicate illustrations)

INDEX